Play
Like
Sergio
Garcia

Play Like Sergio Garcia

AN ANALYSIS OF

THE SWING AND

SHOT-MAKING GAME

OF GOLF'S YOUNG STAR

John Andrisani

G. P. PUTNAM'S SONS · NEW YORK

This book contains an independent study and analysis by John Andrisani, former senior editor of instruction at *Golf Magazine*; he has not consulted with or sought the participation of Sergio Garcia in its preparation.

Outdoor recreational activities are by their very nature potentially hazardous. All participants in such activities must assume the responsibility for their own actions and safety. If you have any health problems or medical conditions, consult with your physician before undertaking any outdoor activities. The information contained in this guidebook cannot replace sound judgment and good decision-making, which can help reduce risk exposure, nor does the scope of this book allow for disclosure of all the potential hazards and risks involved in such activities.

Learn as much as possible about the outdoor recreational activities in which you participate, prepare for the unexpected, and be cautious. The reward will be a safer and more enjoyable experience.

G. P. Putnam's Sons
Publishers Since 1838
a member of
Penguin Group (USA) Inc.
375 Hudson Street
New York, NY 10014

Library of Congress Cataloging-in-Publication Data

Andrisani, John.
    Play like Sergio Garcia : an analysis of the swing and
  shot-making game of golf's young star / John Andrisani.
        p.   cm.
    Includes index.
    ISBN 0-399-15152-4
      1. Swing (Golf).   2. García, Sergio, 1980– .   I. Title.
  GV979.S9A527   2004   2003047188
  796.352'3—dc21

Printed in the United States of America
10 9 8 7 6 5 4 3 2 1

This book is printed on acid-free paper. ∞

Book design by Deborah Kerner/Dancing Bears Design

I dedicate this book

to a younger generation of golfers,

looking to learn how to develop

a unique, natural-feeling,

easy-to-repeat swing technique

that produces powerful on-target shots—

like the ones Sergio Garcia hits.

Contents

1 • El Niño   *2*

The evolution of Sergio Garcia—
from boy wonder to modern-day superstar.

2 • What Matters Most Is Results   *42*

Sergio's swing is unorthodox,
but so was Ben Hogan's.

3 • Far and Away the World's Best   *72*

When it comes to hitting imaginative super-shots—
from the tee, fairway, rough, and trees—
no golfer beats Sergio.

Foreword

Sergio Garcia, four years Tiger's junior, is one of the finest golfers in the world. He's so powerfully accurate that he's led the total driving statistics on the PGA Tour. He's an extremely creative shot-maker. He possesses an outstanding short game that reflects his superb imagination and the influences of such greenside wizards as fellow Spaniard Severiano Ballesteros.

What's so ironic is that when I first saw Sergio play a few years ago, I believed there were elements of his golf swing that could be problematic. In fact, here's an excerpt from an article I wrote in *Golf Digest* magazine:

"Sergio's swing has similarities to the swing of the late Ben Hogan, whom many consider the best ball-striker of all time. But Hogan had better impact alignments. Hogan had incredible clubhead lag, but Sergio is on the verge of having too much."

Quite recently, I was asked to analyze this superstar's swing a second time for *Golf Digest,* and boy, did I notice a difference. Sergio hits the ball longer and straighter, showing what a wonderful job his father, Victor, has done improving his son's swing, particularly relative to reducing the degree of lag in the downswing. This fault is the reason Sergio's game runs hot and cold. But boy, when he's on he's really on, and most of the time he is, which is what any golfer asks of this game.

In observing Sergio, it's quite striking to see the difference between his fundamentally sound setup position and his very personalized backswing and downswing actions. Still, there is a lot you can learn from reading about Sergio's swing and shot-making game in this wonderful instruction book from John Andrisani. I've known John for about twenty years now. John and I have worked together on magazine articles about the swing, and also on instructional books, so I know firsthand that he is one of the true pros in the writing business with a great understanding of golf technique. Therefore, I'm not surprised that he's worked his magic again with the publication of *Play Like Sergio Garcia,* a book that will help golfers of varying handicaps.

This book offers innovative tips based on John's expertise in analyzing the techniques of Sergio Garcia, a golfing dynamo who drives the ball great distances and hits amazing shots—like the huge cut he hit around trees and onto the green during the 1999 PGA Championship. No true golfer will ever forget that shot!

What makes this book even more special are the photographs, especially the one of Sergio swinging at age three, along with those wonderful "takes" appearing in the special eight-page insert. These photographs, showing Sergio's unique technique, will make it easier for you to understand what makes this young superstar's technique tick and also serve as your visual guide to improvement.

Jim McLean
Miami, Florida

• Introduction

Not since I collaborated with Severiano Ballesteros in 1988, on *Natural Golf*, was I so excited about writing an instructional golf book. Coincidentally, Seve is also Spanish and was a young superstar, too, just like Sergio Garcia. Furthermore, sportswriters questioned Seve's unorthodox methods, just like they did Sergio's, until this young golfing genius did the very same thing his fellow countryman did what seems like a century ago: He silenced the critics with his swashbuckling shot-making style, incredible touch, record scores, and winning record.

In *Play Like Sergio Garcia*, I analyze Sergio's tee-to-green game and, with the help of top teachers, tour pros, and true golf experts, offer alternative methods for playing golf.

At the risk of sounding pompous and self-serving, I think it's due time someone offered new instruction to struggling golfers around the world. After all, regardless of sophisticated golf technology, innovative swing analysis machines, an increasing number of golf instructors and golf schools, the advent of The Golf Channel, new golf magazines featuring pages and pages of instruction, and hundreds of golf instruction books flooding the marketplace, the majority of golfers are still failing to improve.

What's so great about Sergio's game is that his shot-making techniques, though unorthodox, work, and work well, because his swing is fundamentally sound. Sergio's grip is neutral, his driving setup is perfectly square, he stays balanced throughout the swing, and, most of all, he repeatedly returns the clubface to a square position at impact.

Golf Digest teaching professional Hank Haney went so far as to say this:

"Of all the recent young phenomenons, Sergio Garcia is the most advanced I've ever seen at playing the game—that is, at understanding different shots, managing them, and controlling his game on the course."

It's Haney's comment that lets you know it is not just Sergio's super swing that is impressive. Rather, it is Sergio's command of the total game, including his course management skills. Sergio's game is so solid that former world-number-one-ranked golfer Greg Norman said: "Sergio has the talent to lead both the American and European PGA Tours."

In *Play Like Sergio Garcia,* I present an in-depth study of how this five-foot-ten-inch, 160-pound twenty-four-year-old generates power. But I also trace Sergio's golf development process, revealing what I believe are his secrets to hitting superlative long and short shots. Also, I analyze his pendulum-style putting action, his practice habits, and his course management game. Having worked on articles and books with golf's greatest players, and teed it up with many of them, including Sergio's golf idol, Severiano Ballesteros, I can say honestly that this youngster from Castellón, Spain, impresses me the most. I truly believe Sergio has the potential to rule the golf world.

If you already follow golf, you know that Sergio Garcia is a player who is exciting to watch and learn from. If you are new to the game, you will also enjoy learning how to drive the ball powerfully and accurately and hit super shots Sergio's way.

Good luck in your quest to improve at golf, and enjoy the game more than ever.

John Andrisani
Sarasota, Florida

Play
Like
Sergio
Garcia

1 ● El Niño

The evolution of Sergio Garcia —
from boy wonder to modern-day superstar.

Sergio
Garcia,
nicknamed El Niño,
is a familiar face
in the golf world,
because of his
exceptional shot-
making skills,
super-energized
competitive spirit,
and winning record.

He learned golf as a young child. He dominated the amateur circuit. He won pro tournaments shortly after turning professional. He drives the ball 300 yards, is super-accurate to boot, and when, on occasion, he misses a fairway or green, he shows his creative genius in recovering. He plays fantastic trouble shots, pitches, chips, and bunker shots. He holes out pressure putts to win big matches. He possesses a positive mental attitude and craves the winner's circle. Golf fans love and respect him for sharing his emotions and exhibiting Superman-type golf skills. He appears on the covers of golf magazines and in television advertisements for golf and non-golf products. He is good-looking and single. Huge galleries follow him at tournaments to see him "go low" and light up the scoreboard in red numbers, signifying under-par scores.

Talking about Tiger Woods? No. I'm describing the youngest superstar on the PGA Tour—Sergio Garcia (aka El Niño)—the twenty-four-year-old golf virtuoso from Spain who, as a boy, played against older players for a Coke or ice cream, then went on to compete against the best players in the world for much bigger prizes.

In a head-to-head match in 1998, billed as the "Battle at Bighorn," Sergio beat chief rival Tiger Woods. Most recently, he proved to the public and press that his victory against Tiger was no fluke. In the 2002 Ryder Cup, Garcia teamed with Lee Westwood and played phenomenal golf to beat Woods and partner Mark Calcavecchia, helping to set the scene for an eventual European victory.

Sergio has sure come a long way in a very short time, which surprises some golf experts, such as Craig Kann of The Golf Channel.

*Sergio with Tiger Woods, the world's number-one golfer,
whom he beat in the one-on-one "Battle at Bighorn."*

"It's hard to believe someone so young is so high on the world rank-ing," said Kann.

Of course, Sergio's major championship record does not stand up to Tiger's, which, as even Sergio admits, is nothing less than phe-nomenal. Yet let's not forget that Woods is four years older than Garcia. So the question is: Who will follow Tiger? George Peper, the former editor-in-chief of *Golf Magazine,* answered that question, as did Geoff Bryant, president of the United States Golf Teachers Federation, and NBC golf commentator Jimmy Roberts.

"No one of any age plays with more feel, finesse, or fervor than Sergio Garcia," said Peper. "Unquestionably, he has the magic touch to dominate the game."

Said Bryant: "Sergio Garcia is the chief threat to Tiger's domi-nance. What makes him so special is that his technique is so similar to Hogan's, but in many ways more refined. For this reason, you have to think he's on the verge of doing something momentous in golf."

Said Roberts: "Sergio Garcia has the talent to be the best golfer in the world."

ROOTS

Sergio Garcia was born in Castellón, Spain, in 1980.
The son of Victor Garcia, teaching professional at Club de Golf de Mediterraneo in Valencia, Sergio began swinging man-size clubs at age three and imitating his father's setup, swing, and shot-making techniques. Because these clubs were cumbersome, Sergio was forced to make compensations for an overly flat swing so that he could return the clubface to a square impact position and strike the ball solidly. Learning to play golf with non-custom clubs should

have been a drawback, but seemingly destiny, or *destino* as the Spanish say, was on young Sergio's side. But there were other critical factors that allowed young Sergio to turn a disadvantage into an advantage. He was blessed with the gift of genius, there is no doubt, but hours and hours of practice and perseverance played their part, too.

One compensatory move Sergio employed involved rotating his left hip briskly counterclockwise at the start of the downswing. Instinctively, he did this to stop being blocked out by his body when delivering the club into impact and, presto, he had found a way to open up a clear passageway for the club to swing on the correct path, directly into the back of the ball.

According to writer Kevin Cook, Sergio made other compensations for his small stature and oversized clubs that proved to be serendipitous.

"Always a bit of a runt, Sergio compensated with a bullwhip motion, delaying the release of the clubhead until the last split second, for power that helped him outdrive grown men," wrote Cook in *T&L Golf*.

By some fluke or act of faith, or because it felt natural, the more Sergio played the more he mimicked the swing movements of legendary pro golfer Ben Hogan, who dominated the game thirty years earlier by employing an unorthodox action that produced super-controlled, powerful shots.

"Hip action funnels the force (golf club) toward your objective (golf ball)," Hogan wrote in his best-selling instructional book *Five Lessons: The Modern Fundamentals of Golf*.

"It puts you in a strong hitting position where the big muscles in the back and the muscles in the shoulders, arms, and hands are properly delayed so that they can produce the maximum performance at the right time and place (impact)."

*Sergio started the game very young,
learning to play golf originally
through trial and error.*

While Sergio was improvising and developing his own personal touches as a golf artist, figuratively speaking, his father made sure his son kept the brush on the canvas. Victor Garcia, being a golf aficionado, knew that as good as Hogan was, his setup was anything but classic. Hogan held the club with a weak grip, set up with his hands a couple of inches behind the ball, positioned his feet "closed," or aiming right of the target, and played from an extremely wide stance. These highly unorthodox elements of the setup were things Hogan did to prevent a hook shot and, instead, promote a very controlled left-to-right fade shot that he felt more comfortable hitting. The trouble is that a Hogan-like setup can lead to problems. Besides, the fade is a weaker shot than a draw, so Garcia Sr. had to go down a different road in training his son.

Garcia Sr. obviously figured out that in order for Sergio to build a unique swing and shot-making game, he first needed to establish a firm foundation. To do that, Sergio had to learn to set up to the ball according to tried-and-true basics, while at the same time incorporating personal nuances into his starting position in order to feel comfortable. These idiosyncrasies included gripping down on the club a couple of inches for added control, setting his right foot dead square to the target line to help create torque in the swing, and positioning his left foot practically perpendicular to the target line to help him hit against a firm left side.

Fortunately, Sergio's father was experienced enough to know that the only way you can get away with an unorthodox backswing and downswing is to start from a square address position. Oh, some of you will argue with me and cite exceptions to the rule, such as legendary player Lee Trevino, who aimed his body well left at address, and you would be right; partially right, anyway. What you fail to realize is that Trevino also aimed his club left of target. So essentially, Trevino set up square, but simply aimed left to allow for his bread-and-butter fade shot that he hit by looping the club back and through and working his body in a way that no one in the world of professional golf had ever done before or has done since. In finishing off my argument concerning why I favor a square setup like Sergio's over an open or closed address position, I quote the great Jack Nicklaus, who wrote the following in his magnum opus instructional book, *Golf My Way*.

"There are some good reasons for my being so methodical about my setup. I think it is the single most important maneuver in golf. It's the only aspect of the swing over which you have one hundred percent conscious control. If you set up correctly, there's a good chance you'll hit a reasonable shot, even if you make a mediocre swing. If you set up incorrectly, you'll hit a lousy shot even if you make the greatest swing in the world."

If you trust Nicklaus, the man who has won more major championships than any other golfer, and you read between the lines, you will realize that a good setup position is what allows Sergio to swing so very differently from any other player, including Ben Hogan, whose technique was similar but not the same. Frankly, no past or present player swings like Sergio. And though, admittedly, he's been criticized, as time goes by and he continues to mature as a player and capture more and more tournaments, the golf world will *know* that his swing is the action of the future—especially since he recently fine-tuned it.

In reading this book, you are a step ahead of your fellow amateur golfers, most of whom struggle with their golf games because they start from a faulty address position and try to perfect a swing that's unnatural. You will benefit from modeling your setup after Sergio's, since each and every element—including grip, stance, ball position,

*Every amateur golfer should copy Sergio's square setup position,
since it promotes a technically sound on-plane swing and
square clubface-to-ball contact at impact.*

posture, body alignment, and clubface aim—is a building block for learning how to swing naturally.

SERGIO'S SETUP

Grip: Sergio sets his hands in a neutral position when holding the club to hit any standard tee-to-green shot. Only when playing some kind of specialty shot, such as a power cut, does Sergio change his grip slightly, moving his hands closer to or farther from the target. It's no coincidence that Sergio's father, who is good enough to compete among the big boys on the senior tour, uses a neutral grip, too, except when curving the ball from the tee, the fairway, or trouble.

Sergio holds the club with a Vardon overlap grip, popularized by six-time British Open winner Harry Vardon during the late 1800s and early 1900s, and now used by all but a couple of PGA Tour players. When gripping, Sergio's right pinkie overlaps his left forefinger, as opposed to the interlock grip, in which these two fingers intertwine. Most good golfers agree that the overlap grip provides a stronger sense of unity between the hands and reduces slippage during the swing, namely because the left forefinger stays wrapped around the club handle.

Although Sergio's grip can be considered classic, he does do one thing very differently from his fellow professionals. Rather than press the thumb and forefinger of the right hand together lightly, as Hogan did, and the majority of pros that prefer to hit a fade do today, Sergio maintains pressure between the tips of these two fingers.

"Gripping the club like Sergio makes much more sense to me, because the two-finger 'squeeze' allows you to use your natural right hand to control the movement of the club and more easily hit a right-to-left draw like Sergio," said John Anselmo, Tiger Woods's former longtime golf instructor. "This feature of Sergio's grip also prevents him from turning his hands into a strong or weak position, which is a common fault among amateur golfers."

Many high-handicappers hold the club with their hands turned well to the right (away from the target, in a strong position), or well to the left (toward the target, in a weak position). These types of grips should be used only when trying to curve the ball dramatically from right to left or in the opposite direction, or when playing a very creative shot around the green.

The majority of country club golfers also grip the club either too lightly, which causes them to lose control of the club, or so tightly that they tense their muscles, which, in turn, causes them to lose all feel for the clubhead and fail to swing the club on the correct path, at a high enough speed to accelerate the club powerfully through the ball in the impact zone. In both cases, the player hits an off-line shot.

Smart golfers, who eventually evolve into low-handicap players, pay close attention to the grip, knowing it truly is the "engine room" of the setup position. To ensure that your grip is neutral like Sergio's, be sure that the Vs formed by your thumbs and forefingers point midway between your chin and right shoulder, and unless you have small hands like Jack Nicklaus and Tiger Woods, use the overlap grip.

For your swing (particularly the downward motion) to essentially work automatically, as Sergio's does, there has to be an even compromise between underactive and overactive hands. So don't choke the handle and deaden the hands or hold the club so lightly that you give your hands too much freedom. When gripping the club to play any standard shot, hold it with a pressure of 6, if on a 1–10 scale 1 is super-light and 10 is super-tight. To check that you're on the right track, ask a friend to pull the club out of your hands. If you are gripping the club correctly, he should feel a bit of resistance. If you're

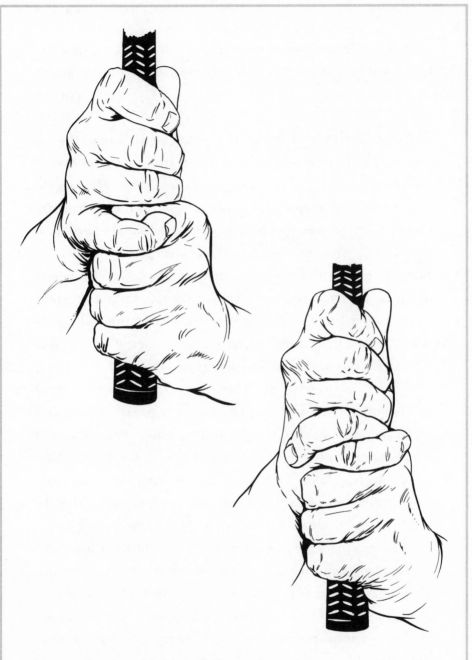

Sergio prefers the overlap grip (left) over the interlock grip (right), because it provides a stronger sense of security and balance in the hands.

gripping too tightly, your friend will need to tug on the club, too lightly and he'll take the club out of your hands with the greatest of ease.

Body Alignment: Whenever I watch Sergio set up to the ball, I'm impressed by the manner in which he gives himself ample time to jockey his body into a square position. He does not rush through his setup routine, as is the case with high-handicap players. When preparing to hit a standard metal wood or iron from the tee or fairway, Sergio sets his feet and body parallel to an imaginary line running from the ball to the target (the target line). Setting up square encourages him to start the club back straight along the target line for about the first foot of the takeaway, then deliver it down the line through impact, so that the center of the clubface contacts the back center portion of the ball.

Evidently, Sergio's father was very strict about the importance of establishing this type of starting position. I imagine this was because Victor Garcia got tired of seeing golfers at his home club hitting bad shots because of a bad setup and didn't want the same thing to happen to his son. I know I get frustrated witnessing golfers hit weak, off-target shots due to a poor setup, as do many instructors I spoke to. There's no excuse for not setting up square to the target line.

The typical amateur aims his feet and body either well left of the target (open alignment) or well right of target (closed alignment). These open and closed positions are okay if you're planning to hit a curving shot around a sharp dogleg hole, or shaping the ball from trouble. But these positions are not recommended under normal circumstances.

When you take an exaggerated closed setup, the tendency is to overturn the hips and swing the club on an overly flat plane. Golfers who turn their hips too much clockwise (more than 45 degrees), and direct the club far inside the target line, destroy their chance of building resistance or torque between their upper and lower body and creating power as a result. Those players who set up closed to the target and swing the club too far behind their body also tend to have trouble squaring up the clubface at impact. They either hit the ball well right of target or, fearing this shot, exaggerate hand action and hit a big hook.

When you start from an exaggerated open setup, the tendency is to pick up the club quickly in the takeaway, swing back outside the target line, and cut across the ball at impact. The end result: slice shots off the tee and fat irons into the green.

To a large extent, body alignment determines the path the club swings along and the shape of the shot you hit. So if you're looking to hit consistently accurate shots that find the fairway or finish next to the flagstick, be sure to groove a square setup like Sergio's.

Clubface Alignment: Sergio aims the clubface square to the target when preparing to hit a straight shot, in sharp contrast to average golfers.

The typical club golfer sets the clubface left or right of the target due to faulty hand position. Whereas Sergio lines his hands up with the ball at address, average golfers position their hands either a couple of inches behind the ball, which forces the clubface to point left, or a couple of inches ahead of the ball, which forces the club to point right of target.

Appreciate how the position of your hands affects clubface position. Understand, too, that a square clubface position at address helps you return the clubface to a square impact position without making any mid-swing compensations.

Sergio is so savvy that he sets the club down square to the target but with the ball fairly close to the heel of the clubhead. This position is not taught to students, yet I believe it is actually one of Sergio's secrets to accurate ball-striking with woods and irons, and something he obviously learned growing up, through hours and hours of experimental, solitary practice.

Teaching guru Phil Ritson, who was the first teacher to spot this nuance, told me that there is actually a method to Sergio's apparent madness.

"Sergio's setup is square but anything but textbook when it comes to setting the club down behind the ball," said Ritson. "The thing is, setting the club behind the ball, with the ball closer to the heel of the clubhead than the center of the clubface, makes sense. That's because as the left hip clears on the downswing, the club actually slides back a fraction toward the body. The bottom line: Playing the ball near the heel means impact will occur closer to the clubface's center, commonly called the sweet spot, which is every golfer's ultimate goal."

Posture: Sergio's posture at address is comfortably correct. His feet are shoulder-width apart, his weight is evenly balanced on his feet and legs, his knees are flexed slightly, and he bends over at the hips, rather than the waist, so that a 30-degree angle is created between the legs and spine. Equally important, Sergio stands close enough to the ball to feel in control and far enough away to give his hands and arms the freedom to swing the club in a relaxed, tension-free manner.

Average golfers, on the other hand, tend to either stoop over at address, which is a position that promotes a very steep plane, or stand practically erect and too far from the ball, which is a position that causes an overly flat swing. So that you don't fall into one of these bad habits, review your posture on video or have your local professional check that you are setting up like Sergio.

"Sergio's postural position will ensure that you stand the right distance from the ball and enable your body to turn more freely going back and coming down into the ball," said Mike Austin, one of golf's premier instructors.

"Work hard on improving posture because it is infinitely more important than most golfers think it is. Take note of your ball flight, too. If you hit low hooks, you're probably standing up too straight. If you tend to hit fat iron shots and pull-slice tee shots, you're probably bending too much at the waist and knees and hunching over at address."

Ball Position: On standard full shots with the driver and fairway metal clubs, Sergio positions the ball somewhere between his left heel and left instep, and that gives him some leeway. The fact that Sergio's ball position varies slightly and is not fixed tells me that he shares the philosophy of Seve Ballesteros, who told me this when we worked on the book *Natural Golf* and he was playing better golf than anyone in the world.

"Some days my body and the club move more slowly than on others, in which case I'll position the ball farther forward to give my sluggish body more time to square up the clubface at impact. Conversely, on mornings when I feel extra-supple and my swing speeds up, I compensate by positioning the ball a little farther back, which helps me stay behind it through the hitting area."

Although Sergio is not so cut-and-dried about ball position, I've observed that he is extremely cautious about the degree of his parameters, making sure not to move the ball beyond his left instep–left heel boundary. High-handicap golfers, on the other hand, frequently miss the mark when positioning the ball, which is a chief reason they are inconsistent ball strikers who often miss their target.

Sergio moves the ball back slightly in his stance as the clubs get shorter in length and more lofted. Yet in playing any full shot he always plays the ball forward enough to ensure a clean sweeping action.

The typical amateur golfer moves the ball so far forward in his stance that he is late in releasing the club and hits a thin slice. Other players tend to move the ball back too far, causing a steep swing and a fat shot.

Drum it into your head that the setup revolves around ball position and the swing revolves around the setup. If you believe your shot-making problems are caused by a fault in ball position, heed the advice of British golf teacher John Jacobs. He recommends that you swing every wood and iron club in the bag, and determine where the clubhead contacts the grass. These spots—opposite the left heel, midway between the feet, etc.—should be your ball positions.

In analyzing Sergio's setup, you can see the influences of his father. While Sergio's love for golf grew stronger, Victor Garcia refined his son's setup and overall action to make them run as effortlessly and efficiently as possible. Although Sergio's swing is similar to Hogan's, there are subtle differences, too, as you will soon realize, owing to differences in their starting positions. It's obvious that Victor Garcia did not allow Sergio to copy Ben Hogan's weak grip, closed stance, and hands-behind-the-ball address position. That was a good thing. Sergio's setup allows him to get in better positions than Hogan and hit the ball even more powerfully and accurately than his professional predecessor. Sergio is such a good driver of the ball that he always finishes high up in the PGA Tour's total driving statistics list, which combines power and accuracy. In fact, he led this category in 2001.

"Sergio Garcia is virtually the same height and weight as Hogan, but he hits the ball a lot farther because his swing positions flow better and require far less manipulation of the club," said Rick Grayson, one of *Golf Magazine*'s top teachers in America.

"I'm more impressed with Sergio's accuracy than his power, his ability to hit a controlled draw rather than a controlled Hogan-like fade," said instructor Miro Bellagamba of the United States Golf Teachers Federation. "The reason is any player who can consistently hit a controlled draw has to swing with wonderful timing.

"Make no mistake, Sergio's tempo is fast, but because his setup is so fundamentally sound he can afford to employ an unorthodox action and swing at high speed yet stay on course. The clubhead never leaves the perfect path."

The combination of good setup fundamentals and idiosyncratic swing actions reminiscent of Hogan's allowed Sergio's game to improve at a very fast rate. At age twelve, he won the club championship at his father's club. Two years later, after developing a well-rounded, extremely creative shot-making game, he became the youngest player ever to make the cut on the European PGA Tour. When he was fifteen, he regularly shot scores in the 60s and became the youngest player ever to win the European Amateur championship. At seventeen, he shocked the golf world by winning a professional event, the Catalonian Open. Sergio's amateur career reached a peak when he won the 1999 British Amateur, thanks to a solid wood and iron game, an uncanny ability to get the ball up and in from around the green, and a fiery competitive spirit.

Sergio rejoices after sinking a winning putt in the final round of the 1999 British Amateur championship (top), then celebrates his victory with his father, Victor Garcia (bottom).

DRIVING, WEDGE PLAY, PUTTING: THE GUTS OF THE GAME

Growing up, Sergio was encouraged to practice drives, wedge shots, and putts, which is anything but a surprise considering that his father was very familiar with something Hogan once said when renowned writer Herbert Warren Wind asked him to name the three most important clubs in the bag. He answered: "The driver, the wedge, and the putter." As a matter of note, the late, great teacher Harvey Penick, author of the best-seller *Harvey Penick's Little Red Book,* gave Wind the same answer when asked the same question.

I'm going to delve deeply into the workings of Sergio's driver, wedge, and putting game techniques in the upcoming chapters. All the same, let me explain why these clubs are so vital to scoring, while at the same time giving you insights into Sergio's game.

Driver: The original name for the driver was the Play Club, which is befitting even today because Ben Hogan's statement made during the 1950s, "If you can't drive the ball, you can't *play* golf," still has merit.

I think what Hogan meant is this: Because the driver is the club that you hit your first shot with on all or nearly all par-four and par-five holes, it is a vital link to playing your best golf. In short, if you are accurate off the tee, you'll be able to play your approach from a clean fairway lie and hit an aggressive shot. If you're a powerful driver as well, you'll be able to play a shorter, more lofted club into the green, which is a big advantage. This is because the short irons are easier to control, so the odds of hitting your approach onto the green, then scoring par or birdie, are increased.

Sergio has always practiced drives (above), wedge shots (facing page, left), and putts (facing page, right), realizing that these three departments represent the guts of the game.

Conversely, if your drives fly wild and not very far, you'll be hitting out of rough or trees and miss the green, and need to depend more on your wedge and putter.

The irony about golf is this: The majority of amateur players are obsessed with hitting drives—only drives—as hard and far as they can. Sergio never fell into the trap of practicing only the driver and concentrating only on hitting the ball as hard as he could. That's because his father obviously drummed home this point repeatedly: *Distance is no good without accuracy.* You, too, should let your buzzwords be *controlled power,* since it is far easier to shoot at the flag from the short grass than the long grass, especially if your drive finishes far down the fairway.

Wedge: It's evident from watching Sergio play short shots so well that he learned the importance of good wedge play at a young age and practiced hard to learn new shots.

Frankly, being good with a wedge is like having a life preserver when you're stranded at sea. The wedge helps Sergio save par, and it will help you, too, if you miss the green or fall short of the putting surface. That's not to say that the wedge should be perceived solely as a bail-out club. It's also a club that will allow you to hit second shots close to the hole on short par-four holes, or third shots stiff to the stick on par fives. It also comes in handy on short par-three holes, when you need to knock the ball in close to set up a birdie putt and take control of a weekend match.

Putter: I have talked a lot about scoring pars and birdies, yet I have not once mentioned the putter, the third most important club in your bag.

The crazy thing about golf, a factor making it both fun and frustrating, is that a drive hit 300 yards and a putt tapped into the cup from an inch away both count as one stroke. Sergio's father knew this fact only too well, and evidently passed on this knowledge. This explains why Sergio spends so much time working on reading greens, practicing his putting setup, and hitting both long and short putts. What's more, he grinds mentally, taking time to access the line and make smooth practice strokes before actually hitting the ball. Of course, I can't possibly read Sergio's mind when he's going through his practice routine. But based on my experience as a former teacher and golf instruction writer, I think Sergio imagines the ball going into the hole to raise the level of his confidence and relax his nerves. I also believe each time he makes a practice stroke, he increases his feel for the correct path of the putter and the speed of the stroke. This is Sergio's way of practicing intelligently. He does not want to miss a putt by inches and then have to count that next short tap-in as a stroke. You won't want to either, so my advice is to learn Sergio's putting secrets, contained in chapters four and five.

HIGHER EDUCATION:
LEARNING FROM TWO GOLF LEGENDS

Sergio's driving, wedge play, and putting skills, together with his work ethic in practicing what his father taught him, allowed him to develop at a fast rate. However, fellow Spaniards Seve Ballesteros and José María Olazabal also helped Sergio become a better golfer.

Ballesteros, who learned the game initially with only a three-iron, explained to Sergio how practicing with one club, hitting shots out of all kinds of lies, and constantly changing elements of the setup, such as ball and hand position or the position of the clubface, enhance your shot-making imagination and allow you to develop

*Advice from fellow Spaniard and short-game wizard Severiano
Ballesteros allows Sergio to hit super shots like this one
from around the green.*

an arsenal of shots. This advice, as well as the wedge game and putting techniques Sergio learned from observing and conversing with Olazabal, turned him into a terrific short-game scrambler. The added bonus of developing a well-versed short game: You can be aggressive on approach shots and attack the flag, knowing if you miss the green you will feel confident about saving par with a good chip and putt.

Sergio's knack for getting the ball up and down, together with what he learned from these two big guns about driving strategy during practice rounds for the 1999 Masters, allowed him to finish low amateur in this prestigious championship that year and gain so much confidence that he turned pro shortly after the tournament.

RISING TO THE OCCASION: SERGIO'S SHOT HEARD AROUND THE GOLF WORLD

The 1999 PGA Championship proved to be a crossroads in Sergio's career, because on the 16th hole of the final round he hit a true miracle shot. With the ball sitting in between the roots of a tree that blocked his line to the hole, it seemed Sergio had no choice but to chip the ball out sideways onto the fairway. Think again. Sergio took out a six-iron, aimed 20 yards left of the tree, and sliced the ball onto the green. I'll analyze how Sergio played the six-iron slice shot in chapter three, so you can learn to curve the ball around trouble—of course, not exactly like Sergio, since this author and many other experts call that shot the greatest shot they've ever seen. In fact, the buzz caused by that shot turned Sergio into an overnight star, even though he lost to Tiger Woods by a stroke. Still, becoming the youngest runner-up in the history of the PGA, at nineteen,

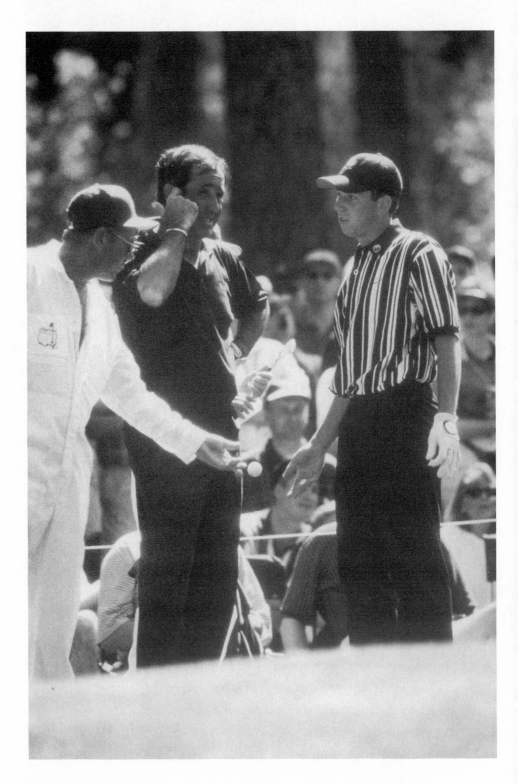

Ballesteros, one of Sergio's chief mentors, offers on-course advice during a practice round at Augusta National, home of the Masters (facing page), then watches as his protégé follows instructions to the letter (above).

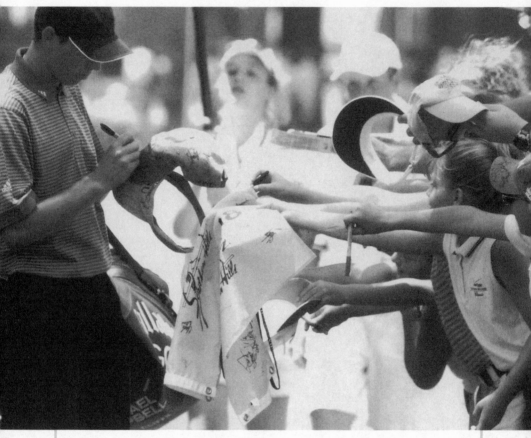

*Sergio, one of today's most popular players,
signs autographs for his fans.*

raised Sergio's confidence level so much that later that year he won the Irish Open and German Masters tournaments on the European PGA Tour.

LOWS AND HIGHS:
SERGIO LEARNS FROM HIS MISTAKES

As good as 1999 was to Sergio, 2000 was not so good. He failed to win a tournament and the American press jumped all over him. They criticized Sergio for taking too much time to start the swing and blamed his father. If people cared they would have discovered that Sergio's slip in the standings was not a slump. He was merely working hard to make some subtle changes in his technique, ideally to raise his game to an even higher level, just as Tiger once did with coach Butch Harmon. Reportedly, Sergio was working hard to reduce the number of times he milked the grip; exaggerating this swing trigger can cause players to tense up golf muscles and lose clubhead speed, or snatch the club up on too steep a plane. In addition, Sergio worked on firming up his wrist action at the top, since over-hinging the wrists on the backswing is likely to cause you to release the club too early on the downswing, or "cast," as teachers describe this fault. Last, he returned to Spain to correct an exaggerated lateral slide of the hips on the downswing, which is a fault that can disrupt balance and cause the clubface to be delivered to the ball in a very open position, and cause a slice or a shot pushed to the right.

Sergio, like all popular players with hectic schedules and endorsement commitments, also needed to spend some quality time away from the game, relaxing with friends and doing some of his favorite things—going to the movies, kicking a soccer ball around, or nightclubbing.

*Sergio's father helps him firm up his backswing position (top)
and swing more rhythmically into a balanced finish (bottom).*

The press can be brutal when desperate for a story, yet the attacks were short-lived. At the start of 2001, Sergio told reporters his father was his only teacher and the one he trusted most. He then proceeded to win his first American PGA Tour event, the Colonial Invitational, shooting 63 in the final round. Next, Sergio poured salt into the wounds by taking home the trophy in the Buick Classic, played over the very demanding Westchester Country Club outside New York City, and beating Tiger by twelve shots with a record 72-hole score of 268, sixteen under par. To cap things off, Sergio also won the Trophée Lancôme in France and the Nedbank Golf Challenge in South Africa. What a year—a true 2001 space odyssey.

In 2002, Sergio got into high gear early, winning the Mercedes Championships, open only to the former year's first-place finishers in PGA Tour events. Starting slowly with a 74, Sergio then shot scores of 67, 68, and 64 to force a playoff with David Toms—which he won after sinking a 10-foot birdie putt on the first sudden-death hole. Suddenly, the press recognized the Spaniard as a genuine star, as evidenced by comments such as this, written by Clifton Brown in *The New York Times.*

"Only a few days before his 22nd birthday, Garcia has cemented his place among the world's best golfers. For Garcia, it was the latest statement that his game is maturing, and that his immense talent is blossoming."

This statement of Brown's proved to be prophetic. Not only was Sergio the only player to finish in the top ten of all four major championships (eighth in the Masters, fourth in the United States Open, eighth in the British Open, and tenth in the PGA), he proved a major force in the Ryder Cup, capturing three points for his European team, which beat the Americans 15½–12½.

One of the chief reasons for Sergio's resurgence in 2001 and 2002 had to do with the mental side of golf. He stopped getting so

Sergio cools out by returning home to Spain for breaks and acting like a kid again. Here, he works out with a soccer ball.

wrapped up in the seriousness of the game that he burst at the seams emotionally, as he once did during the World Match Play Championship, contested at the Wentworth Club in Surrey, England. After a bad, off-balance swing, Sergio pulled off his shoe and kicked it violently.

To show you that Sergio's golf game is no different from yours or mine, in early 2003, after a top-ten finish in the American Express Championship, his game went south again. There was speculation that his new TaylorMade clubs were the reason he started missing fairways, greens, and putts. However, there was no evidence to support those claims. Besides, Sergio would never have switched to those clubs in the first place if he did not think they would help him perform better. Others speculated that his relationship with tennis star Martina Hingis sent him off track, but I wrote this off, too, simply because they saw each other for only a short time.

Sergio admitted to the press that he was working on his swing again, but I really don't think that was the main reason for the downturn. Pro golfers, Tiger included, are always fine-tuning their technique. I believe that fatigue played a role, due to constant travel and meeting the demands of new sponsors, even though Sergio did not admit that. You just cannot think clearly and physically perform to the best of your ability when you are tired. I also believe Sergio needed to go back to the drawing board and work, once again, on anger management. After three-putting holes 9 and 10 during the second round of the 2003 Masters and taking himself out of contention after once holding the lead, he became furious and threw his putter at his bag. From there things got worse, and that's when I think Sergio realized he had to follow in Tiger's footsteps. There's nobody better than Tiger at forgetting a bad shot or a bad hole and turning things around by channeling anger into positive energy.

Instead of losing his temper (above), Sergio now funnels his anger into living a shot through body English (facing page, left) and channeling his energy into fighting determination (facing page, right).

Since that Masters, Sergio's game has returned to form, and here's my take on why. Sergio has become a mature golfer who stays cool on the course. This once somewhat immature and precocious young man has grown up before our eyes. He has finally realized that golf is a lot like life: Some days you get out of bed feeling great, hit every shot perfectly in practice, then play poorly on the course. Other days, you feel sluggish in the morning, hit the ball poorly on the driving range before your scheduled round of golf, then shoot a super score. Like the game of life, the game of golf is unpredictable and cannot be mastered. The secret is to make as few errors as is humanly possible, and to learn from experience.

It's great to see a revitalized Sergio, whose goal is to become the number-one golfer in the world. Many experts predict he will accomplish his goal, thanks to a new mental attitude and a perfected great swing that I'm now going to analyze.

Sergio makes a symbolic statement by climbing to the top of this high hill in the Spanish countryside with a golf club in his hands: He wants to be king of the golf world.

Why Sergio Is Such a Great Golfer

Sergio's father, Victor Garcia, taught him to stick to a set of proven setup fundamentals.

. . .

Sergio was allowed to incorporate personal nuances into his technique, instead of being forced to swing according to a popular method.

. . .

Sergio competed regularly during his youth against older golfers, for a Coke or an ice cream, and these experiences trained him how to play under pressure.

Sergio understood early on that the driver, wedge, and putter are the three most important clubs in the bag, and practiced hard to perfect each.

• • •

Sergio learned the art of imaginative shot-making by

observing fellow Spaniards and golf legends Severiano Ballesteros and José María Olazabal play innovative shots, particularly from around the green.

• • •

Sergio learned to control his anger and stay cool on the course.

• • •

Sergio worked doggedly to perfect his golf swing.

2. What Matters Most Is Results

Sergio's swing is unorthodox,
but so was Ben Hogan's.

Sergio Garcia is one of the world's most powerful and accurate golfers. For this reason, he's capable of driving par-four holes as he does here.

Throughout golf's history, the majority of multiple major championship winners have employed unorthodox swings, proving that you don't need a pure, textbook setup and swing to hit good golf shots.

Jack Nicklaus, the golfer of the century, with more majors to his credit than any other player (eighteen), cocked his head just before triggering the swing, swung the club back on a steep plane, and used violent leg action to start the downswing.

Arnold Palmer's swing was basically a grooved slash.

Gary Player kicked his right knee in at the start of the backswing, then rotated his right side so vigorously on the downswing that he practically fell off his feet.

Before these players, there was Gene Sarazen, whose swing was so rounded it looked like he was swinging inside a giant soup bowl; Walter Hagen, whose technique resembled Babe Ruth's baseball swing; and Ben Hogan, who got so fed up with old-hat instruction that he developed his own unorthodox swing that earned him the reputation of being the ultimate control player.

Even Tiger Woods, winner of eight major championships, does not swing entirely by the book. The trouble is, he is exceptionally flexible and very strong, almost superhuman. So the average player can't really learn to swing anything like him unless numerous hours of leisure time are made available for hitting practice balls, working out, and taking lessons from a golf professional.

One criticism I have of today's top teachers is that too often they believe in just one method for everyone and force a student to learn it. The student then suffers by not being allowed to make the most of his individual strengths, even though he may end up achieving all the precise angles and positions the teacher holds as gospel. Remember this: You don't have to look pretty to play good or even great golf. All you have to do is repeatably apply the clubface squarely to the ball. In fact, as different as the swings of those champions cited earlier are, and those employed by many other players, they all look virtually the same at impact. However, most have to work much harder than Sergio to square the clubface because their backswing movements are unnatural. Sergio's swing is odd, yes. Yet in the words of Butch Harmon, Tiger's teacher, Sergio accomplishes the goal every golfer strives to attain: "He returns the club to the address position at impact and repeats that action consistently."

In analyzing Sergio's swing, inside and out, I've come to the conclusion that the main reason he finishes so high on the statistics list is because his unorthodox backswing is so natural it requires less hand and wrist manipulation to set the club in a good position at the top of the swing and deliver the clubface squarely and solidly into the ball at impact.

"Sergio is really golf's ideal swinger because he mixes solid setup fundamentals taught to him by his father with unique swing keys he taught himself," said Gerald McCullagh, one of the game's most highly respected teachers.

Those unique swing keys allow Sergio to swing the club powerfully, as teaching expert Hank Haney pointed out when analyzing Sergio's swing for *Golf Digest*.

"Sergio also has a lot of power in his swing. He creates tremendous clubhead speed with his big shoulder turn on the backswing and the lag he maintains on the downswing."

When I watch Sergio in action, it's apparent that one of his chief mentors, Severiano Ballesteros, told him what he once told me when we played together at Spain's LaManga Golf Club, and Sergio obviously listened.

"Once you ingrain the proper preliminaries, and get a basic picture and sensory feel for motion, either from a teacher or from watching fine players, then you can tinker with various patterns and combinations of preparation and action until you find your swing, which means the one that is both fundamentally sound and suited to your own build, strength, flexibility, hand-eye coordination, agility, and temperament."

Sergio's wonderful mix of solid fundamentals and personalized swing elements allows his swing to function very efficiently and operate essentially on automatic pilot. Conversely, the mechanical player, who has to think more than feel, must work extra hard to develop a swing, hit the ball well for any length of time, and maintain a robot-like technique. Another advantage of swinging naturally like Sergio is that you will find it much easier to sense a fault and fix it fast and also become a shot-making virtuoso. Also, a natural swing makes you so sensitive to the movements of your body and the club that you can easily make adjustments, such as leaning precisely 60 percent of your weight on your left foot to hit a punch shot or pushing the club back slightly outside the target line to hit a cut. You'll appreciate what I mean more clearly when reading chapters three and four, covering the subjects of long-game and short-game shot-making, and when I teach you how to clone Sergio's techniques. But I'm fast-forwarding. Let me first review Sergio's natural, easy-to-repeat swing, since I believe it's the action of the future—one that will trigger a paradigm shift in golf instruction and allow average golfers like you to finally improve.

It's ironic that Sergio's setup is so fundamentally sound, yet his backswing and downswing are so very extraordinary—reminiscent

Sergio's backswing is unique, particularly the laid-off position of the
club at the top, but it works wonders on the course—
and that's what counts!

of Hogan's but better still. I find Sergio's unorthodox movements very refreshing, considering the cookie-cutter swings of his fellow pros. Had Sergio's father encouraged him to swing by the book, it would have been as tragic as making Picasso paint by numbers. That's because Sergio is as much of a genius with a club in his hands as Picasso was with a paintbrush.

THE BACKSWING

Right from the get-go, when Sergio makes the transition from address to takeaway, we start seeing evidence of his very personalized technique, yet it is one that's so natural, easy to repeat, and effective that all golfers should learn it or switch to it.

Sergio swings the club straight back initially, then inside the target line like the majority of top-notch golf professionals. But he does not use the stronger left arm and left shoulder muscles to control the action, as they do. Sergio is a rebel in this regard, one who disregards the common tenet "Swing the club back in one piece." He pulls on the club gently with his right hand—the same one he uses to turn a doorknob, pick up a coffee cup, hold a tennis racket. This is a big reason why Sergio's swing will feel so natural to right-handed players. Sergio's right-handed takeaway also sets the scene for an eventual wrist hinge that, in turn, removes tension from the arms. Relaxed arms promote more clubhead speed, which means this is one of Sergio's secrets to hitting the golf ball powerfully.

Another unique element of Sergio's takeaway action is that he ignores another so-called basic of golf technique: "Turn the hips clockwise as much as possible at the start of the swing." Like Ben Hogan, Sergio delays this action, actually locking his hips as his shoulders turn and the club is pulled gently back—first along the target line, then on a slight inside path. This is something you don't see other professionals doing, but copying Sergio will enable you to build torque into your swing, which is a very vital link to creating power.

Like the great Jack Nicklaus, who was also criticized for employing an unorthodox golf swing, Sergio starts rotating his chin away from the target early on in the takeaway, to make room for his left shoulder to start turning under it and trigger a weight shift into his right foot and leg. You'll see as we get deeper into this chapter that there are other advantages to head movement. But right now, let me continue describing Sergio's supreme swing technique in sequential order.

Because Sergio's right foot is positioned perpendicular to the target line, and he maintains the flex in his right knee, he reaps the rewards of a solid foundation to swing from. Sergio creates even more torque and power due to increasing resistance between the upper and lower body. Granted, Sergio has to start coiling his hips once weight shifts into his right leg, in order to make room for his arms and hands to swing the club back freely. All the same, Sergio's braced right side serves as a governor and prevents his hips from over-turning. As a result, the smooth tempo, timing, and rhythm of Sergio's swing is maintained. Furthermore, Sergio's braced right knee enables him to extend the club back, and this is one of his secrets to creating an extra-wide swing arc.

At this stage in the swing, other classically trained players let the right elbow fold and tuck into the right side of the body. Sergio, whose father allowed him to improvise, obviously figured out through trial and error that an early folding action of the right elbow is often a direct cause of picking the club straight up into the air and swinging on an upright plane, creating a narrow swing arc and loss of power. If you tuck your right elbow in tight to your body, you'll be able to hit a fade more easily, and be good out of rough, too, because of your steep action. However, you will not be able to hit a powerful draw like Sergio's—a shot that good golfers like to hit because the right-to-left over-spin imparted to the ball promotes added roll and longer drives.

Look carefully at Movement Three in the insert and you'll see how Sergio's right elbow is straight, extended but relaxed. This allows him to maintain a wide arc and promotes a flatter swing path necessary for hitting a draw.

Sergio keeps both hips locked until the clubhead swings well past his right foot and starts moving upward for the very first time, due to a slight hinge in the right wrist. This right wrist cock action, though very slight, allows Sergio to feel the clubhead, giving him an advantage over other players who lock their wrists during the takeaway. Rest assured, you will also add value by allowing your right wrist to give quite early in the swing. You will release any tension in the arms, swing the club up and not around your body, and feel where the clubhead is, which is important in making a timed swinging action.

Though Sergio believes in the freedom of wrist hinge, he does not immediately let his right wrist hinge fully. Anytime you let that happen, you lift the club up abruptly on too steep an angle, narrow the arc of the swing, and lose power.

While Sergio's club does start moving slowly upward at the start of the swing, thanks to gentle hand action, it's also being pushed back well past the right side of his body. So the club is really pushed up and back, rather than merely up, until his hands reach waist level.

Most golf teachers and PGA Tour players believe that you should keep the hands and wrists absolutely quiet in the early stages of the swing. Furthermore, you should use your arms and shoulders to push the club away and let the hands go along for the ride. Sergio breaks these rules. Obviously there is a method to his madness, namely, he wants to feel the position of the clubhead, which is "the starting point of a good golf swing," according to world-renowned teacher Jim Flick.

Teachers can talk all they want about using the big muscles of the body to trigger the swing. However, they had better not speak when Sergio is hitting balls because he'll prove them wrong. The "lightness of being" certainly applies to Sergio's early backswing because it's his relatively light grip pressure, wrist flexibility, slow body movements, and soft hands that make sure the club is pushed back and up until weight starts shifting into his right foot and leg. This pushback action of the clubhead with the hands is the secret to creating a wide swing arc and stretching the muscles of the shoulders as they continue turning clockwise against resisting hips.

Increasing the width of the swing and the degree of shoulder turn are two vital links to swinging powerfully, especially if you take things to the extreme like Sergio. Sergio's arc is super-wide because he keeps his left arm straight, not stiff and tense like many amateurs do. He also promotes power by keeping his hips taut and feet planted firmly on the ground as he swings into a braced right knee. These swing keys also help prevent Sergio's body from swaying, and aid his balance. Sergio's moves contrast sharply with those of the typical amateur player on the backswing. Mr. Average makes a lateral bump with the hips and comes out of his knee flex, which gets him into trouble.

"I cringe when I see a player sway off the ball in an attempt to make a conscious weight shift into the right side," said John Anselmo, Tiger's former teacher. "That's because when you sway you feel you have to make up ground on the downswing by vigorously shifting the hips laterally. And when you do that, you get way ahead of the

MOVEMENT ONE

Sergio Garcia's masterful, melodic, and mega-powerful golf swing

· IN PICTURES ·

AN ANALYSIS OF HIS MAGICAL MOVES

"Sergio's takeaway action is true poetry in motion, proving that all great players build speed gradually, whereas high-handicap golfers tend to jerk the club back quickly, then decelerate through impact."

—**JIM McLEAN,** *GOLF DIGEST* **TEACHING PROFESSIONAL**

"In this position, Sergio proves the importance of coiling into a braced right knee. This is the best way to create power in the swing. Sergio's move contrasts sharply with that employed by the average amateur golfer, who straightens the right leg on the backswing, which is a sure way to cause power to be drained from the swing."

—GEOFF BRYANT, PRESIDENT OF THE UNITED STATES GOLF TEACHERS FEDERATION

"Here we see signs of Sergio's genius. Instead of letting the right elbow fold and tuck early, as so many recreational golfers have been trained to do, Sergio keeps the right elbow extended—one secret to creating a wide and powerful swing arc."

—JOHNNY MYERS, ONE OF *GOLF MAGAZINE'S* FIFTY BEST TEACHERS IN AMERICA

"Sergio's club points left of target, in an unorthodox laid-off position, but so did Ben Hogan's when he swung back to the top. Since Hogan is regarded as the game's all-time best ball-striker, let's just leave it at that."

**—RICK GRAYSON, ONE OF GOLF'S GREATEST TEACHERS
AND AUTHOR OF *SUPERGOLF***

"This is an exceptionally strong power position triggered by a hips-toward-target move. This action prevents the upper body from uncoiling early, thereby making you poised to employ a super-powerful, late hand-arm-club release through the ball—not release the club early, or cast, as many amateurs incorrectly do."

—MIKE LOPUSYNSKI, ONE OF *GOLF MAGAZINE*'S
TOP ONE HUNDRED TEACHERS IN AMERICA

"This square power position of Sergio's happens because he rotates the shaft on the downswing, so the knuckles of his left hand turn to the ground through impact. Most golfers, on the other hand, keep their knuckles pointed to the sky through impact, which causes an open clubface, added loft, and restricted clubhead speed."
—**ROBERT BAKER,** *GOLF MAGAZINE* **MASTER TEACHING PROFESSIONAL**

"When you see the ball zoom off the clubface and fly at the target, as it does here, you know that Sergio got all his previous positions right. By the same token, when you see a high-handicapper's shot slice, you know the player swung the club on a faulty path and plane."

—MIRO BELLAGAMBA, MEMBER OF THE UNITED STATES GOLF TEACHERS FEDERATION

"This classic, full finish position proves that Sergio uncoiled his body so power-fully that he was pulled through the ball. Amateurs get so caught up in trying to hit the ball hard that they lose their balance and hit a wayward shot."

—JOHN ANSELMO, TIGER WOODS' FORMER LONGTIME GOLF INSTRUCTOR

ball, come into impact with the clubface open, and hit a shot well right of target.

"The problem is one of communication. Players and teachers talk too much about shifting weight to the right foot, instead of telling a student to balance his or her weight on the right foot. That's what I taught Tiger and look what he's accomplished."

What really is fascinating about Sergio's backswing action is that once he starts coiling his hips clockwise—and that's not until his hands reach chest height—he uses a "classic turn in a barrel body action," to quote Martin Hall, one of America's top teachers. It's this wind-up action that allows Sergio to boost the club upward easily without consciously pulling its handle upward. The sensation is similar to a sailboat getting help from wind. I say this knowing if you let the hips turn freely the whole swing experience feels effortless.

The turn-in-a-barrel concept involving the hips, as opposed to shifting them laterally first, then twisting them, was dreamed up by Percy Boomer, an Englishman who was the Duke of Windsor's teacher. Boomer would have admired Sergio's backswing pivot action of the hips. To understand the magnitude of what he meant by turning in a barrel, here's what he said in his classic book *Learning Golf*, circa 1946.

"To pivot correctly, imagine that you are standing in a barrel hip-high, big enough to be just free of each hip and just close enough to allow no movement except the pivot."

To accommodate the turning action of his shoulders on the backswing and to further ensure a solid weight transfer, Sergio allows his head to rotate to the right. He does not keep his eyes fixated on the ball, as do many amateurs. This does not bother Sergio in the least, since he knows the ball gets in the way of a good swing, and that you are not required to hit at it. In fact, he does not see the driver actually contact the ball because the downswing takes only one-fifth of a second.

Locking your head on the backswing is actually a fault because it plays havoc with your turning action. What's more, if you lock into the ball with your eyes on the way down, you will tend to decelerate the club at impact and hit at the ball rather than through it.

Jim McLean, who has studied Garcia's swing, is all for the Spaniard's moving his head 20 to 25 degrees. That's because McLean believes the head has to move or the pivot will be tense instead of free-flowing and you will employ a mechanical rather than an athletic swing.

The late, great Harvey Penick went so far as to say: "Show me a player who doesn't move his head and I'll show you someone who can't play."

As Sergio completes the extension action of the hands and club, his shoulders and hips really begin to coil, setting off a chain reaction. The right wrist hinges, the right arm bends at the elbow, the left knee moves inward behind the ball, and the club starts moving behind him. All the time this is happening, Sergio keeps his left heel planted. If you are flexible enough to leave the left foot on the ground, that's good, because you will increase the torque between your upper and lower body and create power. If you feel compelled to lift your heel a little, that's okay, provided you don't lift it so high that you completely deplete your torque established via a strong body twist, or what some teachers call "rotation power."

"You may not be able to turn back as far as I do or keep your left heel down, but try to feel the twisting in your lower body—ankles, knees, and hips," said Sergio in the May 2003 issue of *Golf Magazine.* "The more tension you feel in your legs at the top, the more zip you'll have at the ball."

Some experts, including top teacher Robert Baker, believe Sergio is pound for pound the game's longest hitter. This is due largely to the torque he builds between his upper and lower body and the differential between his shoulder and hip turns. To put things in perspective, Tiger turns his shoulders 120 degrees and his hips 60 degrees, for a differential of 60 degrees. Sergio also turns his shoulders 120 degrees but his hips only 45 degrees, creating stronger torque and more power owing to a gap of 75 degrees. Jim McLean calls this gap the X-Factor because imaginary lines drawn across the hips and shoulders form an X. No Tour player's X-Factor is as big as Sergio's, which explains why this guy of average height and weight smashes the golf ball a country mile.

While the club moves upward, Sergio lets his right elbow move away from his body or "fly." The flying elbow position, popularized by Jack Nicklaus during the 1960s, feels much more natural than trying to keep the elbow close to the body. This unique feature of Sergio's action also prevents him from steepening his swing plane and hitting fat irons and sliced tee shots. It also helps him swing the club into a laid-off position, where the clubshaft points left of target. For these reasons, I'm surprised more and more teachers are not recommending that students mimic Sergio.

Sergio's club is in what's called a laid-off position at the top of the swing—a no-no according to the golf book of basics that calls for the clubshaft to be parallel to the target line.

Try letting your right wrist hinge slightly, swinging on a flatter plane, and letting your right elbow fly away from the body, and you'll match Sergio's backswing position, which is guaranteed to feel more natural and help you make a stronger upper-body coil and hit the ball longer.

There's another very distinct advantage of swinging back like Sergio. You will automatically drop the club into the ideal shallower

Sergio (above) employs a stronger turn than the legendary Ben Hogan (facing page), and because Garcia lets his right elbow fly farther from his body than Hogan did, he swings the club on a wider arc. These are two paramount reasons why Garcia creates much more power on the backswing than Hogan did.

plane once you trigger the downswing (see Movement Five of the insert) and be perfectly poised to swing through in a more stream-lined fashion. You will not need to manipulate the club with your hands to put it into the perfect hitting slot, as so many high-handicappers are forced to do, owing to bad previous positions.

Sergio has also been criticized for his backswing position being compact and well short of the parallel position. But, in actuality, he is ahead of his time. His impressive driving statistics tell you that. In addition, a recent study conducted by renowned teacher Don Tra-han and a team of scientists proved that you can generate as much or more clubhead speed using a three-quarter swing rather than a full swing. This is certainly true in Sergio's case, because his shoulder turn is so strong—even stronger than that of Ben Hogan, who also laid the club off at the top but did not let his right elbow fly.

Some teachers believe Sergio pauses at the top. He's too smart to make that mistake, which is my way of telling you that you shouldn't pause either. If you need to pause at the top, then you could just man-ually place the club in the full backswing position and simply swing down from there. But believe me, this downswing-only method would not be nearly as effective as a full start-to-finish golf swing.

"The fact is, it is only an illusion that the club has paused at the top," said Phil Ritson, the instructor best known for giving David Leadbetter pointers early in his career. "While Sergio's upper torso completes its windup away from the target, his left knee already starts to unwind in the direction of the target. This simultaneous movement of Sergio's in two directions actually freezes the clubshaft in place for the slightest instant, hence the appearance of a pause at the top."

THE DOWNSWING

Once reaching the top, Sergio turns his left knee toward the target, which also pulls the right knee into a square position. It is the movement of the left knee during the swing's transition that begins the left side's dominance during the second half of the swing. As Sergio shifts his left knee toward the target, his legs separate a little farther apart, just as Sam Snead's used to do. This leg separation helps create leverage on the downswing that will allow you to strike the ball with more power than you ever dreamed of.

Sergio's left knee starts a chain reaction in which his entire left side takes control of the downswing. This is crucial because it means that his left side will be pulling the club through the downswing, just as the right wrist and right hand did the pulling while the club was moving in the opposite direction. And, as you might remember from your physics classes, any pulling action on an object (in this case, the golf club) is more efficient than a pushing action. This simple law explains why Sergio's right-side-controlled backswing and left-side-controlled downswing—both pulling actions—provide by far the most effective overall golf swing.

Once Sergio triggers the downswing with his left knee, he starts turning his left hip and side in a counterclockwise direction, to his left and rear. Copying Sergio will allow you to start transferring weight to your left foot and leg pivot post.

As Sergio's left hip starts to turn, his arms drop downward, with the right elbow tucking in close to his side. This drop-down move allows the club to fall into a shallower, perfect hitting slot. You want to bring the club into the ball on a shallow angle like Sergio when hitting the long clubs—driver, fairway metal woods, and long

Sergio's secrets to storing power until the last vital moment of the downswing, and setting himself in position to make the hardest possible hit, are dropping the club down into a shallow path and maintaining the hinge in his wrists.

irons—so that you promote a powerful sweeping action through impact.

What's so superb about this stage of Sergio's downswing is that he retains pressure in his right foot and leg, which prevents an over-the-top move so common among club-level golfers. This action also helps him maintain the hinge in his right wrist for most of the downswing. This tremendous lag in Sergio's downswing is his trade-mark, and so impressive that it prompted golf commentator and former golfing great Johnny Miller to make this profound statement during the telecast of the 2002 Ryder Cup: "Nobody since Hogan has the [same] kind of lag in his swing as Sergio Garcia."

Sergio accomplishes lag by pulling on the club handle with his left hand at the beginning of the downswing, with the club's butt end pointing toward the target line. Sergio completes the ultimate power position by rotating his right side into a braced left-leg pivot post while his upper body actually falls back away from the target and his right elbow drops down into his side. This fire-and-fall-back action actually causes a positive whiplash effect, with the hinge in the right wrist increasing and the club gaining momentum as it swings on a shallow and narrow arc. Mike Lopuszynski, one of America's best teachers, who analyzed Sergio's swing for *Golf Magazine*, explains:

"A narrow downswing spells power because it means you've initiated the forward swing by shifting your hips toward the target before the arms and hands start down. This move keeps your upper body coiled like a spring, storing energy and setting up a late release with the hands and arms through the ball, not before impact, as many amateurs incorrectly do."

Sergio's power play is also enhanced by his right elbow and right shoulder, which both drop downward as the body shift occurs. These two simultaneous movements maximize the lag feature in Sergio's downswing, creating even more power.

Popular instructor Robert Baker, who has taught top tour pros such as Ernie Els and A-list celebrities such as Michael Douglas, believes that Sergio's "drop down" downswing, involving the right elbow and right shoulder, together with pulling the club's butt end aggressively toward the target, increases his wrist angle and stores loads of energy in the wrists.

Baker's insights—and he has one of the best pairs of eyes and analytical minds in the teaching world—don't surprise me, considering Sergio's downswing looks similar to the one employed by Ben Hogan. It was Hogan who believed the right elbow was responsible for helping direct the club into the ball at speed and whipping the right wrist back into a straight position at impact. I agree, provided you keep the upper part of your left arm glued to your body like Sergio. By following Sergio's example, you'll guard against throwing the clubhead outside the target line with your right hand, arm, and shoulder and prevent a poorly hit shot.

When the hands drop down into the hitting area, and the right wrist is hinged back, centrifugal force takes over, allowing Sergio to swing through all the individual positions he practiced without thinking about hitting the ball. For any normal full shot, you must not make any conscious effort to hit or add power to the shot through impact.

Once the hands drop to waist level, with the right wrist hinged back, Sergio's shoulders are closed, proving that the lower body leads the downswing. At this stage of the swing, it's no longer a pulling action with the left hand that controls all the action. Sergio simply continues turning his body through the shot. The rotary turn of his hips automatically brings his hands, his arms, and the club-head out and around so that the clubface returns to the back of the ball on a shallow path from inside to along the target line at impact. Any attempt to hit with the hands will only serve to throw away clubhead speed prematurely, as well as increase the chance of delivering the clubhead inaccurately to the ball and mishitting the shot.

As soon as Sergio nears impact and about 80 percent of his weight shifts to his left foot, his right wrist starts unhinging. That's when the club really starts to accelerate, once again thanks to centrifugal force and no conscious manipulation of the club with the hands. Because Sergio properly coordinates club and body movements, you would never know his downswing reaches a speed of more than 120 miles per hour. His swing rhythm is so smooth that he sometimes creates the appearance that he is swinging in slow motion. Here are some tips to help you improve your tempo, timing, and rhythm:

On the downswing, the movement of your shoulders should work in a seesaw fashion. The turning of the shoulders through the downswing, perpendicular to your spine, brings the right shoulder down, under your chin, while the left shoulder works back up. However, instead of forcing your head to stay down as the right shoulder moves past it, it's much better to let your head swivel along with your shoulders through impact. The result will be a much smoother move through the hitting area.

A swiveling head and rotating hips allow Sergio to spring off his right foot and start whipping the club toward the ball.

"The faster the hips uncoil, the faster the arms swing, the more clubhead speed generated, the farther the ball flies," said Jim McLean, a member of *Golf Digest's* staff of teaching professionals.

Unlike the average high-handicapper, Sergio is not anxious to hit the ball. He waits until the hips clear before he lets his right wrist unhinge and really whip the club into impact.

Both Sergio (above) and Ben Hogan (facing page) use the right elbow as a steering wheel, to keep the club on track. But because Garcia holds back the release of his right side longer through impact, he creates more swing torque—power—than Hogan did.

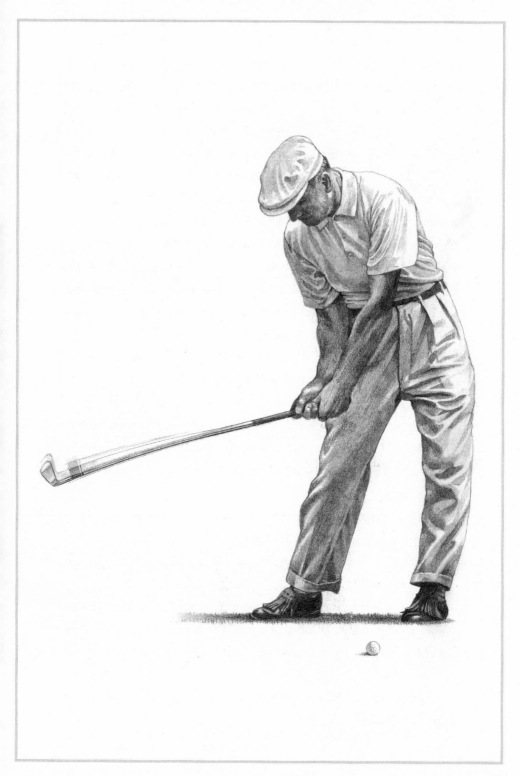

In the hitting area, it's Sergio's left hand that guides the club into the ball, the right hand that provides power. Returning the club to a square position and generating high clubhead speed should be your priorities, too, since both of these elements are critical to achieving clubface-to-ball compression. To compress the ball powerfully, the clubhead must travel low to the ground and straight along the target line past impact, with the clubface staying on the ball a fraction of a second longer. This club-to-ball action pays great dividends because it's been scientifically proven that the longer the ball is compressed, the farther it flies. Sergio is obviously aware of this fact, because the flat spot in his downswing starts from a point several inches behind the ball and ends at a point several inches in front of it. It is, in fact, a feature of his swing that allows him to hit the ball much more powerfully and accurately off the tee than Hogan did during the 1950s when he played his best golf. Hogan held on to the club more firmly with his left hand through impact, delayed the release, and swung down and up rather than down and through. This is because Hogan's goal was to hit a fade. In sharp contrast to Hogan, Garcia's release is full and free because his goal is to hit a dead-straight shot or a slight draw.

Striving for a long flat spot will encourage you to swing the club on a low and streamlined shallow arc and come into impact like Sergio: with the club reaching peak speed at the moment the clubface contacts the ball.

As you can see from viewing Movement Six in the insert, Sergio is in a model impact position, one that you and every other golfer should copy. You will know that by the result: a powerfully hit, accurate shot.

To achieve a good impact position, you must appreciate what is happening in Sergio's swing.

- Sergio's hips are clearing while his upper body tilts
  away from the target.
- Sergio's left arm is extended, while his right arm is bent
  slightly at the elbow.
- Sergio's left shoulder and left hip are higher than his
  right shoulder and hip, ensuring a powerful hit.
- Sergio has shifted the majority of his weight to his
  left foot.
- Sergio's right heel is well ahead of the toe end of his
  right foot, much like Hogan's during his heyday.
- Sergio's right knee has rotated inward and toward
  the target, indicating that he rotated his right hip
  counterclockwise.
- Sergio's left arm and clubshaft form a straight line,
  proving that he maintained constant grip pressure
  and kept his upper left arm close to his chest.
- Sergio's clubhead is low to the ground, proving that his
  angle of attack was shallow.
- Sergio's clubface is dead square to the target, indicating
  that his clubhead path was correct and there was no
  exaggerated manipulation of the club handle with
  his hands.

In sharp contrast to high-handicap golfers, who let the left arm
bend dramatically, or "chicken wing," through impact, jut the right
shoulder outward from the body, and bring the club across the target
line, Sergio synchronizes his club and body movements in an exceptional manner. His arms stay close to his body and his hips uncoil
fully, which help him direct the club squarely and solidly into the
ball and down the target line. His right wrist straightens at the precise

Sergio's "flat spot" (above) is longer than Ben Hogan's (facing page), which is why Garcia hits the ball so much longer than his legendary predecessor.

moment of impact, releasing all of his stored energy and whipping the clubface squarely into the ball at high speed. His success supports renowned teacher John Jacobs, who has always said that "powerful shots are the result of clubhead speed correctly applied."

Sergio's follow-through and finish positions are a direct result of previous swing movements and are attained reflexively, but they are anything but irrelevant. In fact, if you form a clear mental picture of Sergio's superb follow-through in your mind before you swing, you will physically swing into, then through, all of the previous vital positions he employs, as easily as connecting dots on a page. Here's what you should look for when analyzing your swing and determining what you need to see in your mind's eye prior to swinging.

In the follow-through, the clubshaft should finish parallel to the target line, with the toe of the clubhead pointing upward. This position proves that you kept the club square to the target at impact and a few inches beyond that point.

Sergio's extended right arm and head-back positions are similar to those employed by Ben Hogan, who also compressed the ball powerfully. However, Hogan set up closed, buckled his left wrist and turned his right hand under his left through impact, arrived at the ball with the clubface slightly open, and hit a fade. Sergio sets up square, turns his right hand over his left through impact, closes the clubface slightly, and hits a draw.

In the extended follow-through position, Sergio's chest faces left of target, proving he rotated his hips in a counterclockwise direction. His eyes look directly down the target line, because he fully rotated his right shoulder under his chin. This is what Claude Harmon, renowned teacher and 1948 Masters champion, told his students is really meant by keeping your eyes on the ball. It does not mean getting stuck in the impact position with your eyes looking straight down at the tee on which the ball was placed.

In the finish, you should be balanced and standing virtually erect with the clubshaft behind your neck. Sergio, like Hogan, finishes in a comfortably relaxed position with all but five percent of his body weight on his left foot. However, Sergio's finish is more low and around than Hogan's because he swings the club more to the inside and hits a draw. Because Hogan hit a fade, his hands finished so high above his head that the clubshaft did not hit his neck. Without a doubt, Sergio is the more natural swinger. Hogan's swing requires much more strength, much more flexibility, and much more practice.

The press and some television golf swing analysts can criticize Sergio all they want. The fact is, you cannot possibly arrive in a super-balanced finish position like his unless you swing at a controlled speed and the sequence of your body movements on the backswing and downswing is synchronized to the letter with the sequential movements of the golf club.

Because the timing and rhythm of Sergio's swing is so good, he'll keep winning tournaments and crying all the way to the bank, and not worry about waiting for the day when so-called experts realize that his action is *the* swing of the new millennium. Before you swing, it will also help to vividly see yourself in Sergio's balanced finish position. So take the time to implant Movement Eight, shown in the insert, into your head, especially the clubshaft-behind-neck position. That's because trying to swing into that position will encourage you to accelerate the club through impact and make solid contact without being hindered by thinking about hitting the little white ball.

Why Sergio Is Such a Great Golfer

Sergio grips and re-grips the club until he feels he's ready, and looks down at the ball and back up at the target until he sees the perfect shot come to life in his mind's eye.

• • •

Sergio's backswing action is natural and tension-free, and he swings the club along a wide arc to create power.

• • •

Sergio maintains the hinge in his right wrist until the last vital moment of the downswing, when he straightens it and whips the club into the ball at high speed.

. . .

Sergio's good sense of balance and superb swing tempo, timing, and rhythm allow him to hit the ball both powerfully and accurately.

. . .

Sergio stands up to every shot confident he will hit a good shot, because he trusts his swing, which is as unorthodox as Ben Hogan's but easier to repeat and more efficient.

3 • Far and Away the World's Best

When it comes to hitting imaginative super-shots —
from the tee, fairway, rough, and trees —
no golfer beats Sergio.

Sergio Garcia has the creativity and skill to hit shots other golfers wouldn't even dream about.

In the history of the game, there have been only a handful of players who are considered true shot-making geniuses with a golf club in their hands. The most legendary shot-makers include Walter Hagen, Bobby Jones, Arnold Palmer, Chi Chi Rodriguez, and Seve Ballesteros. In their heyday, each of these players could work the ball in any direction and on any trajectory—from the tee, fairway, or trouble areas. Surprisingly, Tiger Woods is a supreme tee-to-green player, but he's not considered an exceptional innovative shot-maker.

Already, the world's most formidable tour players, teachers, sportswriters, and television golf analysts have added another pro golfer to this short list of players who can make the ball talk: Sergio Garcia, who said this in *Golf Magazine*:

"I've always been one to play around with different kinds of shots—knockdowns, fades, low shots, high shots—sometimes even when my natural draw would work just fine. But that's all part of maturing as a player. Now I see the right shot, the simplest shot for the situation, more often. But I must confess: I still like to be creative."

Sergio's prowess is quite surprising when you consider his young age. But not at all surprising when you consider Sergio's good schooling, vivid imagination, and superb feel for the golf club, and the super-shots this Spanish superstar has already hit to rewrite the record books. Let's look at these shots, including the six-iron slice that Sergio hit during the 1999 PGA—considered by many golf experts to be one of the greatest golf shots of all time.

QUICK DRAW

This is a drive that turns from right to left, more than a normal draw, and flies lower, too. It's the ideal type of tee shot to hit when playing into a strong wind. The advantage of hitting such a shot is that you will not lose any distance off the tee because of a headwind. In fact, because the ball rolls more upon landing, you can actually gain distance, especially if you turn the ball around a dogleg left.

Sergio depended on the quick draw to beat the wind en route to winning his first PGA Tour event, the 2001 Colonial Invitational contested over the Colonial Country Club in Fort Worth, Texas. Garcia had the quick draw under such control that he shot a last round 63 to snatch the $720,000 first-place check from a strong group of challengers, including Phil "Lefty" Mickelson, one of the world's top tour professionals.

PLAY LIKE Sergio ➡

How to Hit the *Quick Draw*

Sergio tees up extra-high, so that all but one-third of the ball is above the top of the driver's face. This high tee position promotes a flat swing arc, which in turn allows your hands and forearms to rotate counterclockwise quite dramatically through impact. These hand-forearm actions turn the clubface into a closed, toe-leading-heel position at impact. Consequently, exaggerated right-to-left spin is imparted to the ball.

To further promote a more rounded backswing arc, Garcia strengthens his grip. Do this yourself by turning both of your hands away from the target slightly, until the Vs formed by each thumb and forefinger point up at your right shoulder as you set the driver behind the ball. When Sergio sets the club down, its face points well right of target. Follow his example to allow for the quick-turning draw shot.

In order to promote a very free turn of the right hip on the backswing and make room for the club to swing on a flatter plane, Garcia sets up closed. Do this yourself by setting your right foot back a couple of inches from its normal square position. To help promote a wide and powerful swing like Sergio's, stand with your feet wider apart than normal. (Addressing the ball with your feet close together causes you to pick up the club very quickly in the takeaway and narrow your arc, which drains vital power from your swing.)

To further maximize the width of his backswing arc, Garcia moves his whole body laterally from the target the moment he starts the club away. This highly unorthodox swing key increases the distance the clubhead travels, thereby giving Sergio the length of swing arc of a much taller man. Using this method, he's able to hit the ball much farther down the fairway than if he employed the standard swing. If you are shorter than six feet in height, this same move will help you maximize your power off the tee.

When hitting the quick-draw shot, Sergio also rotates his hips more vigorously than the typical PGA Tour player. This is one chief reason that he is able to create tremendous power. If you think locked hips may be restricting your power, let go.

On reaching the top of the swing, Sergio rotates his right hip briskly in a counterclockwise direction. This one action will push your weight back over to your left side and cause your knees to swivel toward the target. In turn, your arms and the club drop into the desired, more shallow power slot.

*When hitting the quick draw, Sergio moves well onto his
right side on the backswing, the purpose being
to create a more powerful swing arc.*

Sergio's incredible arm-hand-body rotation allows him to release the club powerfully through impact and impart exaggerated draw-spin to the ball.

Releasing his right side also helps Sergio clear his left hip more quickly and easily. Once that clearing action is triggered, Sergio's arms extend out at the ball. It's at this stage of the swing that you will probably start feeling the building pulse of power being transmitted through your hands and arms, provided you maintain good balance by keeping your head behind the ball. All of this energized power you create will ultimately be transferred to the clubhead at impact.

When Sergio's hands drop to a level even with his thighs, he begins to rotate his right forearm in a counterclockwise direction. Finally, once Sergio releases his hands and unhinges his right wrist, the club whips into the ball at high speed, with its face closing through impact. Consequently, Sergio is ensured of imparting draw-spin to the ball.

POWER CUT

Sergio depended on this high, left-to-right shot to win the 2001 Buick Classic, played at the Westchester Country Club in Harrison, New York. It came in especially handy on the 15th hole, which turns dramatically from left to right.

The power cut will help you cut the corner of a sharp dogleg-right hole. This is an advantage because by effectively shortening the length of a hole you leave yourself an approach shot with a more lofted club, which is far easier to hit and control than a longer, less lofted club.

Sergio also depends on the power cut when the fairways are fast-running. The advantage of playing this shot is that you can hit the ball higher and with fade-spin so that it will sit down quickly, even on firm fairways.

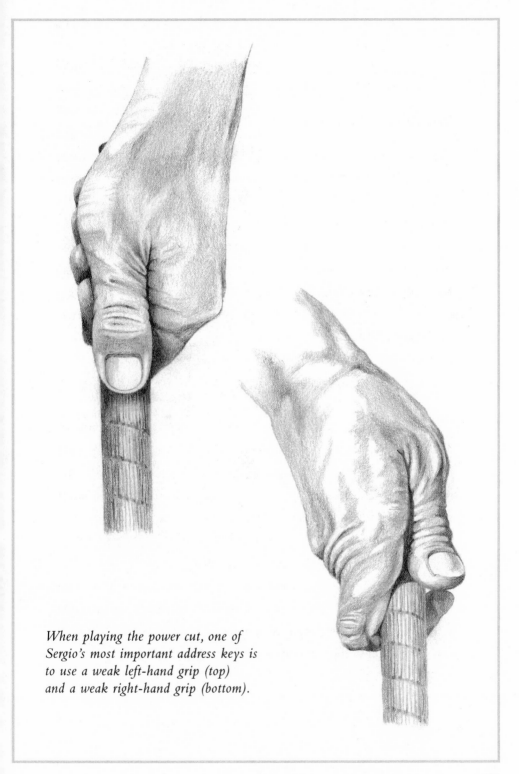

When playing the power cut, one of
Sergio's most important address keys is
to use a weak left-hand grip (top)
and a weak right-hand grip (bottom).

PLAY LIKE Sergio ➡

How to Hit the *Power Cut*

I noticed that in preparing to play the power-cut shot, Sergio tees the ball up lower than normal; the top of the ball is even with the top of the driver's face. This feature of his pre-swing routine may seem minor but in fact it helps promote an upright swing plane. To further promote an upright backswing, set your hands in a weak grip position, so the Vs formed by your thumbs and forefingers point up at your chin.

Another way Sergio prepares to hit the power-cut drive is setting up open. Do this yourself by aiming your feet, knees, hips, and shoulders on the line where you want the shot to start. Next, set the driver face dead square to the target, where you want the ball to finish.

Once Sergio is satisfied that his setup is correct, he swings the club back essentially in his normal fashion, the only real difference being that he holds on a little longer with his left hand in the hitting area to delay the release action of the club. As a result, the club is slightly open when it's delivered into the ball. The shot Sergio produces shoots powerfully off the clubface, curves slightly from left to right in the air, then lands softly on the fairway grass.

Although the power cut seems like a hard shot to hit, it really is not difficult to learn. Just devote some time to practicing the same setup and swing keys Sergio depends on, and I guarantee within a short time you will be able to work the ball to the right.

When playing the power-cut tee shot, Sergio delays the release of the club longer than normal, to ensure a slightly open clubface at impact.

BULLET

When Sergio hits the bullet off the tee, with a three-wood or a two-iron, the ball flies so straight and so far that he's able to sail past other pros and win championships played on extremely narrow courses. Such a victory came in the 1999 Irish Open.

PLAY LIKE Sergio ➡

How to Hit the *Bullet*

Sergio's major address key to playing the bullet is positioning the ball back in his stance with his hands ahead of it. This setup allows you to hood the face at address, which is the position you want to repeat at impact in order to hit the ball on a low trajectory.

Follow Sergio's example of keeping the backswing action as simple and controlled as possible—slow but rhythmically powerful, in an arc that's short but wide. To keep the action compact, minimize wrist action as you extend the clubhead well back along the target line with your arms. To create width, turn your shoulders more than normal.

In swinging down, concentrate on delivering the club on a shallow angle from the inside, then chasing the ball with the clubhead through impact. This mental image will allow you to stay down longer like Sergio, put the sweet spot of the clubface on the ball, and create a longer flat spot with the clubhead in the hitting area. In turn, the clubface will stay on the ball longer, allowing you to hit it more powerfully and accurately.

The shot you hit will bore into the wind and run fast and far down the fairway.

When playing a bullet shot, Sergio swings the club down on a
very shallow arc, promoting an exaggerated flat spot
and extra-low ball flight.

HIGH FLYER

If it weren't for this shot, Sergio would never have shot 64 in the final round of the 2003 Mercedes Championships, and won the tournament played over Kapalua's Plantation course in Hawaii.

What put Sergio in the driver's seat was shooting a 31 on the front nine, thanks to a high-flyer three-wood shot he hit off the fairway turf on the par-five 9th hole that helped him score an eagle 3.

The advantage of hitting the super-high three-wood is that the ball will stop extra quickly on the green. You can also use it from the tee on a long par-three hole, or on your approach to a long par four, or when trying to hit a small, fast-running green on a par-five hole. When Sergio scored the eagle in the final round of the Mercedes, the ball soared high into the air, then dropped down to the green, finishing just three feet from the hole.

PLAY LIKE Sergio ➡

How to Hit the *High Flyer*

When playing this shot, Sergio positions the ball off his left instep and sets about 55 percent of his body weight on his right foot. This setup will ultimately allow you to hit the ball on the upswing and attain the desired high, soft-landing trajectory. Nevertheless, for that to happen, you still must do a couple of other things like Sergio.

On the backswing, Sergio concentrates on keeping his hands away from the body, so that he swings the club more up than around. But you must be careful not to swing the hands too far inside the target line, with your right elbow rotating behind your back, or you will enter what teacher Jim McLean calls the "dead zone"—leaving

One of Sergio's address keys to playing the high flyer is to set slightly more weight on his right foot than his left.

you in an awkward position and unable to deliver the club on the desired path.

On the downswing, Sergio watches the ball a split second longer, which helps him stay down and behind the ball. These are two more technical links to hitting the high-flying three-wood shot.

FAIRWAY BUNKER SWEEP

Thanks to this shot, played from a shallow fairway bunker, Sergio is often able to reach the green of a par-four hole, or get close enough to a par-five hole in two, and still score a birdie. In fact, being such a master of the fairway bunker sweep shot enabled Sergio to win the 1999 German Masters.

How to Hit the *Fairway Bunker Sweep*

When setting up to play the sweep, a cleanly hit solid shot from a fairway bunker, Sergio wriggles his feet into the sand only slightly. You don't want to restrict leg action by digging your spikes deeply into the sand. Sergio also makes sure that he sets his right foot slightly in back of his left foot, in a closed position, to encourage a flat backswing plane. He also balances his weight evenly on both feet and plays the ball just behind his left heel. Guard against playing the ball back in your stance, or else you will dig the club into the sand at impact instead of sweeping it cleanly, and lose distance. Sergio also sets his hands a little bit behind the ball to further promote an upswing sweep at impact. Letting your hands drift ahead of the ball will lead to a choppy action, so pay close attention to this element of the address.

On the backswing, Sergio swings the club just inside the target line to promote a more rounded swing plane and ultimately a sweep action at impact. Further, he rotates his left shoulder fully under his chin to create stored power via a strong body coil.

On the downswing, Sergio drops his right elbow in close to his side so the club drops into a flatter path. You need to make this move and stay down in order to be able to sweep the ball cleanly off the sand. If you want to get a little extra out of the shot, via added roll, exaggerate the releasing action of your right hand and arm through impact. That way, you will cause the clubface to close slightly and impart hot over-spin on the ball.

*Swing down on a flatter path and keep your knees flexed to sweep
the ball cleanly off the sand, as Sergio does here.*

SIX-IRON SLICE

Sergio hit this truly miraculous shot during the final round of the 1999 PGA, contested at the very long and challenging Medinah Country Club in Medinah, Illinois. Trailing Tiger by two strokes, Sergio's drive landed at the base of a tree, in a dirt patch between tree roots, and in a position that blocked his line to the green. It looked like Sergio's charge was finished. Even the most experienced golf aficionados I talked to at the time figured Sergio would be forced to take an unplayable lie penalty drop or to chip out sideways. After all, just putting the club on the ball would be tough, maybe even impossible.

In case you were not lucky enough to witness what happened next, Sergio, to the dismay of the gallery and every television commentator, started looking over the lie and the target in such a serious way that you knew he was going to risk getting hurt, risk missing the ball, and risk making a big number on the hole. The young Spanish superstar was going to try to hit a miracle shot onto the green from 200 yards out. From the glare in Sergio's eyes, you just knew his imagination was running wild and he was playing the perfect six-iron slice shot in his mind, to test out the technique mentally and give himself the confidence to play it physically, as all great shot-makers do.

Sergio pulled off the shot, causing the mouths of fans to drop open, and leaving television announcers speechless, and me and other golf nuts at home going wild, as the shot curved around the tree, sailed low before rising and slicing right, then landed on the green. Sergio scored an unbelievable par four, when it looked like a double bogey was in the cards, and kept his hopes of winning the 1999 PGA alive.

Sergio swings down across the target line to hit the six-iron slice shot, with his hips clearing more than normal in a counterclockwise direction.

The fact that Sergio ended up losing to Tiger is what everyone forgets. All golfers remember is that miracle shot hit by Sergio—one that CBS commentator Jim Nantz called "one of the most remarkable shots in the annals of PGA history."

PLAY LIKE Sergio ➡

How to Play the *Six-Iron Slice*

In setting up to play this shot, Sergio stands more erect with his hands closer to his body and the ball positioned a couple of inches back from his left heel. In addition, he takes an exaggerated open stance, aiming his body well left of the target.

Sergio's setup will help you swing the club on an upright plane and on an out-to-in path, which are two technical "musts" for hitting down sharply and imparting slice-spin on the ball. Still, push the club back outside the target line in the takeaway and set your wrists sooner than normal to make sure you are poised to accomplish your goals. For added control, follow Sergio's example of employing a compact backswing.

On the downswing, Sergio makes a lateral shift with his hips, then clears them quickly. Sergio's hip action helps him swing the club across the ball, while keeping his left wrist arched and turning his right hand under his left hand. This cut-across, turning-under action is what allows the ball to fly high and curve dramatically from left to right.

SOFTY

One of the dangers for pros and amateur golfers is facing an iron shot out of rough. I say this because you always have to worry about the ball flying 10 to 20 yards farther than normal because of blades of grass (or moisture in wet rough) getting in between the ball and the clubface at impact.

The best strategy for countering a flyer lie is to reduce spin and take something off the shot, which is exactly what Sergio did en route to winning the 2001 Lancôme Trophy on the European PGA Tour.

PLAY LIKE *Sergio* ➡

How to Play the *Softy*

In analyzing Sergio's technique, I've noticed that he plays the ball well up in his stance and canters, or tilts, his left hip up slightly. Both of these setup keys help promote an upswing hit and thus allow you to put as much clubface on the ball as possible. The cleaner the hit, the less the ball will fly. Sergio also takes one more club for the distance at hand (i.e., a five-iron instead of a six-iron) to compensate for opening the clubface slightly at address, and because an open clubface and upswing hit cause you to hit the ball on a higher trajectory.

On the downswing, Sergio straightens his left leg so that he's ensured of hitting against a firm left side and driving the clubface under the ball. The last thing you want to do is increase the flyer effect by pulling the club down with your hands and hitting down sharply. Instead, accelerate your arms, then turn your right hand

*When playing a softy shot from rough, promote fluid arm acceleration
and an upswing hit by striving for a full Sergio Garcia–like finish.*

under the left through impact to further increase the effective loft of the club and ensure clean clubface-to-ball contact.

SLIDER

Chances are, you will never play Augusta National, home of the Masters and the course where Sergio used this shot en route to finishing low amateur in 1999. However, you will definitely face a shot over water and sand to a pin cut on the right side of a green. And, too, there will come a day when this situation will be toughened due to wind blowing in your face.

When facing these course conditions, you want to hit the ball on a low trajectory to cheat the wind, and slide it from left to right to avoid the hazards as much as possible. Therefore, follow the example set by Sergio, who plays this shot virtually to perfection.

PLAY LIKE Sergio ➡

How to Play the *Slider*

When setting up, aim slightly left of the hole, at the "fat" of the green rather than the flag. Play the ball back in your stance, with your hands a few inches ahead of it so you decrease the effective loft of the clubface. In addition, place 60 percent of your weight on your left foot to promote a steeper backswing plane and sharper angle of attack.

Make a wide, compact backswing.

Coming down, pull the club through like Sergio does in the photograph on page 94, which shows him hitting a slider on

When he's hitting the slider, all the way through impact Sergio's left hand points in the direction in which the ball will start its flight—left of target—while the clubface points directly at his final target—the flagstick.

Augusta's par-three 12th hole. Also, try to get the back of your left hand to point left of target, where the ball will start its flight. Restrict the release of the club, too, by holding on more tightly with the left hand. I've noticed that this little technical trick of Sergio's allows him to keep the clubface pointing at his final target. Copy Sergio's masterful technique and the ball will slide from left to right.

Why Sergio Is Such a Great Golfer

Sergio's feel for the club-head and understanding of swing mechanics are so good, he has the ability to hit all types of tee shots, including the power cut or low-flying bullet.

• • •

Sergio's good schooling and intelligent practice sessions allowed him to develop such a wide repertoire of shots that he can get out of any on-course jam.

• • •

Sergio can recover from a fairway bunker by making a more rounded backswing, swinging the club down on

an extra-shallow arc, and picking the ball cleanly off the sand.

• • •

Sergio can slice a ball around trees by swinging the club on an exaggerated out-to-in path, as he proved in the 1999 PGA Championship.

Sergio can hit a high, soft-landing shot from rough by swinging the club back on an upright plane, then rotating his right hand under his left through impact.

• • •

Sergio can hit a shot that flies around trouble by the green and slides from left to right at the target by setting up open, making a compact backswing, restricting the release of the club on the downswing, and delivering the club into the ball with its face slightly open.

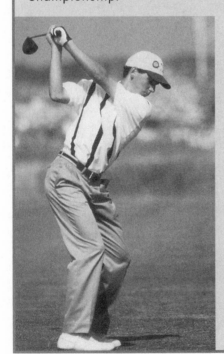

4 • Short and Sweet

What you can learn from
Sergio's creative short-game techniques.

*Sergio
Garcia*
*celebrates after
chipping the ball
into the hole to
win a sudden-death
playoff against
Ernie Els in the
2001 Nedbank
Challenge in South
Africa. What a
short game!*

There is no question that driving the ball powerfully and accurately off the tee sets Sergio up to hit attacking on-target approach shots. Nevertheless, as great a player as El Niño is, he is not so robotic that his swing works each and every time on automatic pilot and produces shots that repeatedly fly at the flagstick and finish next to the hole. No professional is that consistent, simply because the swing itself requires the player to be in full control of the movement of both the body and the club, with the entire action needing to be timed well for a powerfully accurate shot to be hit. One's emotions also play an important role in the execution of a golf shot, as do metabolism and adrenaline. In short, a lot has to go right for any player to hit a golf ball squarely and solidly on all eighteen holes.

Admittedly, Sergio shows qualities of genius when playing golf. He truly is a shot-making virtuoso. Nevertheless, not every shot is perfectly executed. Sergio faces reality and accepts that he is going to hit tee shots off target and miss greens because of a bad swing or a bad bounce. This is precisely why he worked so hard to develop a repertoire of short-game shots that enable him, and will you, too, to save par after one of your shots misses the putting surface and you need desperately to get the ball up onto the green and down into the hole in two strokes.

Sergio's mastery is a tribute to his father, the man who provided him with a good short-game education, teaching him the setup and swing basics for hitting pitch shots, chips, bunker shots, and putts. But, according to my research, tips from two fellow countrymen, Severiano Ballesteros and José María Olazabal, both short-game wizards, together with what Sergio learned on his own through hard practice, helped him develop an array of short-game shots that are as colorful and varied as pieces in a kaleidoscope. In fact, many golf experts believe that when it comes to hitting creative short shots and getting the ball up and in from near or around the green, Sergio is the best of all.

"Sergio Garcia may just be the most imaginative short-game player on the PGA Tour," said Rick Grayson, one of *Golf Magazine*'s top teachers in America.

What sets Garcia apart from other professionals is his uncanny ability to look at a lie, eye up the target, pick the right club, and play a shot he has already hit in his mind's eye. In observing Sergio analyzing a course situation, you can see that he loves the challenge of trying to figure out the best strategy and shot-making choice. What Sergio loves most, though, is playing a spectacular recovery shot that generates loud applause from the gallery or causes golf enthusiasts to stand frozen with a look of amazement on their faces.

It's no wonder that Sergio is often compared to another Spaniard, Picasso, who, just like Sergio, was blessed, learned through experimentation, and depended on deep emotions to drive him. The main difference between these two creative giants: Picasso used a paintbrush to create masterpieces on canvas while Sergio uses a golf club to create masterful shots on the canvas of the course.

Until I first started observing Sergio at the 1999 PGA, I was sure no golfer would ever be better at hitting short shots than Severiano Ballesteros, Tiger Woods, and Phil Mickelson. I won't go so far as to say that Sergio is in another league from these other super-talents, yet I will say that in a contest to determine the best short-game player, Sergio would come out on top. The reason I'm so confident about my selection has mainly to do with pure mathematics. Sergio simply has more shots in his bag. He is a street fighter with a big heart, great hands, and super eye-hand coordination. Sergio is so talented that he almost always finds a way to hit a miracle shot and beat the course.

I am impressed most by Sergio's pitching prowess, which is the department of the game I'd like to analyze first, starting with two shots—the *spinner* and the *parachute*—that he plays from out in the fairway.

The spinner is ideal when hitting a long pitch to a hole situated behind a water hazard or a deep bunker, because you can land the ball as much as 10 yards behind the flag and spin it back. José María Olazabal played this shot quite a bit en route to winning the 1994 Masters, so it's apparent that Sergio learned this technique from observing his fellow countryman.

The parachute is ideal from shorter range, particularly when hitting to a pin 20 to 60 yards away that's situated on a level plateau of a sloped, fast-running green, like those at Royal Lytham & St. Annes, where Ballesteros, Sergio's golf idol, won his third British Open title. When you plug this fact into your brain, you can guess who Sergio learned this valuable greenside shot from. Put this shot in your bag because it will allow you to attack a sucker pin and beat the odds by stopping the ball on the level plateau of a sloping green, leaving you a hole-able putt.

Let's now review these two very different wedge-swing techniques before moving on to the pitch and roll, then analyzing the unique quality of Sergio's chipping, pitching, bunker play, and putting techniques.

PITCHING

PLAY LIKE Sergio ➡

How to Hit the *Spinner*

In setting up with a pitching wedge, play the ball back in a square stance, with your hands a few inches ahead of it. Put 70 percent of your body weight on your left foot and stand closer to the ball than normal, with the toe end of your right foot perpendicular to the target line. Next, cant your hips toward the target slightly and be sure they are parallel to the target line. All of Sergio's setup keys, just reviewed, serve a dual purpose. They allow you to swing the club on a steep plane and make sharp contact with the ball, with no fear of pulling the shot left of target.

Since Sergio's goal is to come into impact using a hit-and-hold action to impart backspin to the ball, he encourages this by weakening his grip. You do this simply by moving both hands toward the target until the Vs formed by the thumbs and forefingers point up at your chin. In preparing to hit this shot, Sergio sets the club down very lightly. That's because he knows that pushing the sole of the club down hard against the turf can cause him to tense the muscles in his arms, lose the feel for the clubhead, and swing on an incorrect path. Follow Sergio's example, and also grip and re-grip a couple of times until you feel your hand pressure is right and you are ready to start swinging back.

In swinging the club back with his hands and arms, Sergio hinges his right wrist early in the takeaway. Giving yourself this same freedom will relieve tension in your arms and hands and ensure that you

*One secret to hitting a successful spinner like Sergio is to
pull the club sharply into the back of the ball.*

swing the club up quite quickly. Remember, you must swing back on a slightly steeper plane than normal to ultimately hit down sharply and impart backspin on the ball.

Since the spinner is usually played from the 75-to-100-yard range, you do not need to generate as much power, via a strong shoulder and hip turn and weight-shifting action, as you do when hitting a long club. Yes, you still should shift weight to your right foot on the backswing, but avoid getting overzealous and exaggerating lower body action. Keep the backswing short and compact like Sergio's, too, since this will aid your control.

On the downswing, shift your weight over to your left foot, then let the large muscles of the left hip, shoulder, and upper arm take control of the action. Once your left hip begins rotating around to the left, pull the club down sharply. But, like Sergio, maintain the hinge in your right wrist until the moment of impact, when the back of the left hand faces the target, the right wrist straightens, and the clubface compresses the ball. This delayed release of the right wrist is the most vital link to imparting maximum backspin on the ball, and no golfer holds the angle better than Sergio.

The "delayed hit" is such a vital key to power that I want to teach you a drill designed to help you ingrain the feeling of holding your right hand back as you approach the hitting area. Phil Ritson, one of golf's premier instructors, invented this "dagger drill." Here's how it works:

Position yourself as if you are halfway into your downswing, with your wrists fully cocked so that the butt end of the club is pointing down at the ball. Now move your right hand onto the metal shaft a few inches below the grip. While holding the shaft back with your right hand, try to pull the butt of the club straight down at the ball. You'll feel the resistance along the outside of your left arm and shoulder. This is the sensation you want to develop in your actual swing. Pull the club down with your left arm leading and keep the right wrist cocked until as late as possible. You should have the sensation that your right hand is chasing your left through the impact zone, with both wrists maintaining the angles that were first established at address.

If you copy Sergio's technique and work on Ritson's drill, you will feel no need to lift the ball into the air. The 52 degrees of loft built into the pitching wedge will do the work for you. The ball will take off a shade lower than it would with your old scooping action. Because of the sharp angle of attack, the ball will rise quickly to its apex, then drop to the green at a steep angle with plenty of spin. Depending on the firmness of the green, and assuming you've played the shot from a good lie, the ball will hit the green and then suck back toward the hole.

PLAY LIKE Sergio ➡

How to Hit the *Parachute*

When preparing to play the parachute with a sand wedge, position the ball forward in a narrow, open stance. Sergio plays the ball off his left instep to help him stay behind the shot through impact and loft the ball high into the air. He sets his feet open slightly, both to limit the amount of body turn on the backswing and to help him more easily clear his left side as he starts down to the ball.

The most interesting feature of Sergio's address, when playing this shot, is his grip. You can tell by how freely he waggles the club that his grip is light, which promotes fluid hand action. The position of the clubface is unique, too. Sergio lays it open slightly to further promote the desired soft-landing ball flight he's looking to achieve.

When playing the parachute, it's critical that you copy Sergio's way of turning the right hand under the left in the hitting area.

On the backswing, Sergio leans left, dipping his left shoulder downward in a kind of reverse pivot that automatically propels his arms and the club upward. As the club swings up in response to the dipping of the left shoulder, Sergio's upper body rocks a little toward the target. By the time Sergio's left shoulder has rotated under his chin and the club has reached the completion of its motion, in a half-swing to three-quarter position, his right leg is firmly braced in a straight up-and-down position, preventing a faulty body sway.

Knowing that his downswing goal is to shovel the clubface cleanly under the ball at impact, Sergio triggers the downswing by gently rotating his knees toward the target, which has the effect of rocking his upper body away from it, or to his right, while at the same time pulling the club downward with his right hand. This miniature reverse pivot, or falling-back movement, allows him to stay well behind the ball, with his weight heavily on his right side. Also, by forcing his left shoulder upward, the action allows his left hand to pass the ball before he slides the clubface under it with his right hand. The shot he hits flies softly and high so that its elevation and steep descent produce only one soft bounce before it "dies" and rolls slowly toward the pin.

PLAY LIKE Sergio ➡

How to Hit the *Pitch and Roll*

When setting up to play this 40- to 60-yard shot off fairway grass, to a hole situated on the upper level of a two-tiered green, pick a landing spot in the clear entranceway leading to the putting surface. Next, imagine the ball hitting the spot you selected, taking one fairly big bounce, then bouncing gently a couple of times before rolling all the way to the hole. Now you've put yourself in the right frame of mind to play this shot. You let your imagination run wild, which is very important for sound execution. Imagining or visualizing the ideal shot before hitting the ball raises your level of confidence and relaxes your muscles. In turn, you are better able to execute the shot using the following technique employed by Sergio.

At address, position the ball just behind the midway point in your stance. Be careful not to move the ball too far back or you will hit down too sharply and make contact with the ball before the clubface has time to square itself to the target at impact. Spread your feet shoulder-width apart and distribute your weight evenly toward the balls of both feet to promote a relatively flat swing plane. To further promote a slightly flatter plane, like Sergio's, stand a bit farther away from the ball with your knees flexed less than normal.

In swinging back, rotate your knees fairly briskly in a clockwise direction, which promotes a full weight shift to the right foot and encourages the arms to swing the club on a somewhat flat plane. Also, delay the hinging action of your right wrist to guard against picking up the club too abruptly. On this shot, Sergio keeps his wrists virtually "dead" and his hands low so that he can swing the club on a shallow plane and sweep the ball cleanly off the turf. At their highest point in the backswing, Sergio's hands are at waist level, the clubface is fanned open, and his right wrist is only slightly cocked.

On the downswing, rotate your knees smoothly toward the target while shifting weight back to your left foot. These two triggers allow Sergio to look effortless when he swings the club back to the target line then along it with his arms predominantly controlling the motion. Finally, through impact, rotate your right hand smoothly over your left hand so you cause the toe of the club to lead the heel and hook-spin to be imparted to the ball.

When hitting the pitch and roll, let your right hand rotate over your
left through impact, so you close the clubface slightly and impart
a slight degree of hook-spin on the ball.

*Depending on the lie, contour of the green, and distance
of the shot, Sergio plays either a running chip
that reacts like a putted ball (above) or a lofted chip
that stops more quickly (facing page).*

Because the downswing plane is shallow rather than steep, the divot is a mere scrape in the grass, something you should look for as a checkpoint. As for the ball, it flies on a low trajectory, lands short of the clear entranceway to the green, bounces a couple of times, then rolls the rest of the way to the hole—just as you imagined.

CHIPPING

When it comes to chipping, Sergio again employs unorthodox yet natural-feeling techniques that vary according to the lie of the ball. Whereas other top pros and teachers recommend that you chip like you putt, meaning that you should employ a dead-wristed/dead-handed stroke, Sergio does not. He hinges the wrists slightly if the lie is good, a little more if the lie is bad, and quite dramatically if the lie is ugly. Sergio also distributes his weight differently and alters his hand and body positions, depending on the course situation. But again, it's his wrist action that is the focal point of his chipping technique, and this makes perfect sense to veteran pro golfer Chi Chi Rodriguez.

"I like the way Sergio chips, because active hands and wrists allow you to better work the clubhead, and thus enhance your feel for playing delicate touch shots," said Chi Chi.

Another glaring difference between Sergio and other professionals is that, rather than use a variety of clubs to chip with, he wields the sand wedge when playing most chip shots. However, he changes the clubface position, usually opening or closing it to change the trajectory of the shot.

To appreciate Sergio's chipping prowess, let's take three common course situations—good, bad, and ugly—and see how he handles each by varying his technique slightly.

SITUATION 1 ... *The ball is sitting up in the fringe grass, approximately 30 feet from the hole, and the green is level.*

PLAY LIKE Sergio ➡

How to Chip from a *Good Lie*

Position the ball midway between your feet, setting them about six inches apart. This narrow stance will make you feel like your entire body is closer to the ball, which increases your sense of being in complete control of the stroke.

Sergio uses a square stance and sets the clubface dead square to the target, since his objective is to swing the club virtually straight back and through along the target line on a flat-bottomed arc. A fairly firm grip will help you accomplish this goal, and gripping down about an inch on the handle, like Sergio, will further enhance your control of the chipping stroke. Flex your knees to establish a solid foundation for swinging. Contact the ball with only a slight descending blow, so complete your setup by putting just a little more weight on your left foot, and set your hands just a fraction ahead of the ball.

Sergio minimizes lower body action as he hinges the right wrist just slightly and swings only his hands back to a point level with his right thigh. You don't ever want to make a long swing when chipping. As the shots get longer, simply hood the face of the sand wedge or take a less lofted club. Sergio never chips with any more than a nine-iron, and I think that's a good idea. When you chip with a very low-lofted club it is very hard to judge the strength of stroke needed to hit the ball the correct distance.

Let your right wrist unhinge and swing the club into the ball using your hands and arms. Because you swung the club on a wide arc and a relatively flat plane, the shot you hit will carry the fringe, land on the green, and roll to the hole like a putt.

SITUATION 2... *The ball is sitting in a threadbare area of fringe 90 feet from the hole, which is situated on a small level area of green above a severe slope.*

PLAY LIKE Sergio ➡

How to Chip from a *Bad Lie*

Sergio sets up open, with the ball positioned near his right foot in a narrow stance and his hands a couple of inches ahead of the clubhead. This address position encourages you to hit down sharply, so you pop the ball out of the bad lie and onto the green.

Swing the club back to waist height, allowing your right wrist to hinge quite early to promote an upright plane that's necessary for bringing the club sharply into the ball at impact and nipping it off the tight lie. It's this nipping action that imparts added spin to the ball. Nevertheless, be cautious not to let the right wrist hinge all the way back or the plane will be so steep you will probably hit a fat shot off this sandy lie.

Pull the club down with your left hand and let the right hand go along for the ride. Also, drive the club low through impact, so you keep the clubface on the ball longer than normal and impart exaggerated spin on it. Do this right and the ball will "dance."

SITUATION 3 ... *The ball is virtually sub-merged in long grass, approximately 15 feet from the hole, and the green is fast.*

PLAY LIKE Sergio ➡

How to Chip from an *Ugly Lie*

In setting up to play a shot out of greenside "junk," Sergio pulls his left foot back a few inches from the square position to give himself a better picture of the line and to provide clearance for his arms to accelerate the club freely through impact. Sergio also opens the clubface and sets his hands slightly behind the ball to program added height into the shot.

Like Sergio, hinge your wrists fully, swing the club slightly out-side the target line, and stop the backswing when your hands reach chest height.

Pull the club down across the line with your left hand, while let-ting your right hand rotate under it. This physical key, plus keeping your head behind the ball, ensures an upswing hit and an open club-face position at impact.

The shot you hit will fly high and fade slightly because a small degree of cut-spin was imparted to the ball, due mostly to swinging the club on an out-to-in path. Once on the green, the ball will spin right and trickle toward the hole.

BUNKER PLAY TECHNIQUES

In talking to private country club and public course golfers, I was surprised how many players experience nervous twitches when facing a bunker shot and, as a result, either top the ball or dig down so deep into the sand that they leave the ball in the bunker. I was even more surprised to hear many players shyly confess to not carrying a sand wedge in their golf bag.

I hope you have a sand wedge in your bag or else you have no chance of recovering like Sergio. I say this because all sand wedges feature a specially designed "bounce" feature that consists of added metal that falls below the clubface's leading edge. This bounce acts as a sort of rudder and thus allows the club to take a shallow cut of sand under the ball rather than digging down deeply in an area behind the ball.

Provided you have a sand wedge, you are now ready to learn how Sergio recovers from a good lie, a bad lie, and an ugly lie in a bunker.

SITUATION 1... *The ball sits atop the sand, anywhere from 25 to 50 feet from the hole. The lie is flat and the ball is a few yards away from the bunker's lip, so it's not necessary to get the shot up extra-fast.*

PLAY LIKE Sergio ➡

How to Hit a *Good-Lie* Bunker Shot

Open your stance about 25 degrees to the left of target. Align your clubface open, pointing it to the right of the hole by about the same amount as your stance points to the left. Your weight should be fifty-fifty between your feet, your stance narrow. The ball should be positioned opposite your left heel so that your hands are just slightly ahead of the ball. Just as a reminder, make sure you have the clubhead above the sand because touching any part of the hazard prior to making a swing will cost you a penalty stroke. This setup position will promote an outside-in swing path through the sand which, coupled with the open clubface, will impart a definite left-to-right side spin on the ball that ensures it will sit softly when it lands.

There are two ways to control the distance you hit a good-lie sand shot. One is to make the club contact the sand a little farther behind the ball for a short shot, or to hit closer to the ball when you need a longer carry. The other way to control distance, and the one Sergio prefers, is to hit the sand the same distance behind the ball every time and use the length of the swing to control the force of the shot. In observing Sergio play out of bunkers, I determined that he hits the same two inches behind the ball on all normal shots, and I recommend you do the same. I think this is the simplest approach and the one that will breed confidence. So focus hard on your contact spot before you swing. (Only when facing an exceptionally long bunker shot, of around 40 yards, does Sergio change his shot-making strategy.)

After looking back and forth from ball to target a few times and waggling the club up and down just as many times, take the club back in a fairly narrow, upright arc and allow your wrists to cock the club upward.

On the downswing, keep your eyes focused on your contact spot two inches behind the ball, where you want the flange of the club to enter the sand. Next, pull down pretty firmly with the last three fingers of your left hand, then try to follow an image of slicing a cut of sand out from under the ball. This will keep the clubface open at

On short bunker shots, the clubhead should finish pointing at the target, with its face pointing toward the sky, as Sergio illustrates here.

impact, so that you get greater loft and cut-spin on the shot. Because the clubhead will meet more resistance in hitting sand on a rather steep downward arc, your follow-through will be restricted, so the club will finish more or less pointing at the target, rather than moving into the complete follow-through position.

If you face a slightly longer or shorter sand shot than the example I've given, again, all you have to do is adjust the length of your swing while keeping everything else constant. For a shot of, say, 20 feet, you won't have to take the club quite to the position where the clubshaft is virtually perpendicular to the ground. If you face, say, a 60-foot bunker shot, you'll probably need to make a full-length swing like the one employed by Sergio.

Whatever the length of shot, keep in mind the firmness or softness of the sand, which can be determined by the feedback you receive when wriggling your feet into the sand. This pre-swing test process should factor into your awareness of how full a swing you need to employ. The fact that Sergio takes his time settling his feet into the sand tells me he thinks hard about the texture, knowing it will tell him a lot about how to play the shot. If the base is shallow, you don't need to generate quite as much force as normal because the flange will "bounce" a little more. There will be less sand between the club and ball and thus less cushion to the shot. If the sand is very soft, more of it will stay between the club and the ball and the shot will come out a bit softer.

As soon as you understand the mechanics of the basic sand shot, it's just a matter of repeating the shot over and over until you can groove the correct action. To expedite the learning process, take a bucket of balls into a practice bunker and spend some time playing basic sand shots. Play a game with yourself in which you must keep playing the shot until you've completed a reasonable goal—say, until you've hit at least five shots within six feet of the cup and five shots within three feet of the cup. Trust me: The hard work and discipline will pay off as it has done for Sergio.

SITUATION 2... *The ball sits half submerged in sand, fairly close to the bunker's lip, and 20 feet from the hole.*

PLAY LIKE Sergio ➡

How to Hit a *Bad-Lie* Bunker Shot

When hitting this shot, the main thing you must accomplish is to get the leading edge of the club under the level of the ball, so the sand pushes the ball forward and out over the bunker's lip. To help you accomplish this goal, move the ball back in a square stance and move your hands forward so they are ahead of the ball.

When watching Sergio set up to play a long bunker shot, I noticed that he hoods the clubface of his sand wedge so it points downward slightly. The main reason for hooding the face is that it lowers the leading edge and eliminates the bounce on the rear of the flange. So the leading edge will dig into the sand more, as it needs to, rather than bouncing off the sand and hitting the top of the ball.

Another vital link to recovering is balancing slightly more of your body weight on your left foot. Distributing your weight this way also has a positive effect on the arc of your swing.

In executing this shot, you must swing the club on a steep arc dominated by your arms. The lean-left address position, as well as playing the ball back with the hands ahead, will help you swing the club up steeply and hit down about an inch behind the ball. Still, it's important to keep your grip light and your wrist action loose on the backswing to ensure a short, steep swing action.

When recovering from a buried lie, with little green to work with, use a firm hit-and-hold action at impact, as Sergio does here.

You'll find that by hooding the clubface the needed amount and using a firm hit-and-hold action at impact, the ball will come out of the buried lie a lot more easily than you think. The only problem is, it will fly out much lower and with almost no backspin, so it will run fairly "hot" after landing. If you've got some green to work with, say, 25 feet or more, you can still hit the ball close to the hole. However, when the pin is tucked close to the bunker's lip, you should play for the fat of the green or employ Sergio's special scoop action.

"Sergio is the only PGA Tour player I've ever seen use this method, taught to me many years ago by the great South African Bobby Locke," said teaching guru Phil Ritson. "Just before Sergio swings into impact, he allows his left elbow to wing or fly out away from the body. This winging action makes the clubhead take out a short, deep scoop of sand with the clubface working into an open position.

"This opening of the face very effectively works the flange underneath the ball, even though it was buried. So when this shot is properly executed, the ball pops out softly. Not only can you hit the ball out, you can hit it stiff to the stick."

SITUATION 3... *The ball lies close to the lip, forty to sixty yards from the green.*

PLAY LIKE Sergio ➡

How to Hit the *Ugly-Lie* Bunker Shot

The farther you are from the hole, the more you should square the clubface of a sand wedge because that's the easiest way to subtract loft from the club as compared to the open position for a basic bunker shot. (If you have trouble reaching the green, consider playing a nine-iron or a pitching wedge. It's good to experiment, but you will probably get the best results using a sand wedge that will not only help you launch the ball to the hole more easily but also make it simpler to play the shot because of its bigger flange.)

In setting up, you should bring your stance closer to square to the target. Also, align your shoulders parallel to the target line, so that your swing force is more directly at the hole, causing the ball to travel farther.

Looking at your contact point, this time only about a half-inch behind the ball, swing the club back on a shallow arc with your arms and hands.

"If you have trouble doing this, follow Sergio's example of holding the club with a strong grip," said Ken Venturi. "I did this throughout my golf career and it really helped me."

Keep your backswing compact, too, in order to guard against over-hinging the wrists, steepening the angle of ascent, and hitting down sharply.

Swing the club down from inside the target line on an even shallower arc, exaggerate your counterclockwise right forearm–right hand release action, hit your designated contact point, and sweep through the sand taking a very thin divot.

If you copy Sergio, you'll hit a low-flying sand shot that lands by the hole and "checks."

To play a long bunker shot like Sergio, be sure to swing down on an extra-shallow arc and exaggerate your right arm and hand release action.

PUTTING

Sergio relates to the emotional swings that occur during a round on the greens, just like you. Putting truly is a game of inches—fractions of inches, in fact. Ironically, some days you putt well during your pre-round putting practice and seem to lose your stroke on the course, while other days you miss practice putts then hole almost every putt on the course. Sometimes you hit bad putts that somehow fall into the side door of the cup, while other times you hit a good putt that veers off because of heavy grain in the grass, a spike mark, or a barely visible imperfection in the green.

What's so crazy about putting is that it requires you to make the shortest stroke of all clubs, yet in between so much can go wrong. Most of the time, mistakes are the result of poor green-reading habits, a lack of confidence, or the anxiety related to the fear of missing a putt that you expect to make. Worrying about shooting your best score or needing to hole a putt on the last hole to win a match also affects one's nerves.

The best defense against poor putting is an aggressive offense. First of all, choose a putter that is aesthetically pleasing to the eyes, feels good in your hands, is well suited to your height and hand position, and helps you employ a technically sound stroke. Second, learn to read the break in a green. Third, set up with the putter's face square to the correct line you've read. Fourth, develop a stroke that allows you to swing the putter straight back and then straight through along the target line on short putts and on an inside-square-inside path on long putts. Fifth, know that the better you prepare, the better your action; the better your action, the more positive your mental attitude; the more confidence you have, the more putts you will hole.

Since Sergio possesses such good putting habits, let's take a look at his setup and stroke action.

SERGIO'S PUTTING SETUP

Sergio's address position is absolutely textbook. This may surprise you, considering that Sergio is a rebel of sorts and that some professional and amateur golfers who are good putters start from an unorthodox address position. Some golfers stand with their feet wide apart, some stoop way over, some set up open to the target line or even closed. The fact is, these same players have been setting up this way all of their golfing lives. Unless you have already grooved a unique setup, you will hole many more putts if you follow Sergio's example.

In setting up, Sergio positions the ball opposite his left heel, the lowest point in his stroke. He distributes his weight evenly on each foot to preserve balance and promote a smooth, well-timed, consistent back-and-through stroke.

Sergio also lines his hands up with the ball, so that the back of his left hand is square to the hole. A common fault among high-handicap players is lining up with the hands either slightly behind the ball or well ahead of it. Lining up with your hands in back of the ball causes you to swing the putter back outside the target line, then across the ball at impact. Setting up with your hands several inches ahead of the ball causes you to pick up the putter on the backswing and ultimately chop down at impact. Either fault will cause you to miss the hole, so be sure to check your hand position in front of a mirror or on video.

Sergio sets his body square to the target line. You are deemed square if imaginary lines running across you feet, knees, hips, and shoulders run parallel to the ball-hole line. Sergio sets the putter's face square to the hole, too, unless the ball is going to break, in which case he sets the face square to the crest of the break, several inches or feet left or right of the hole.

Another element of Sergio's setup that you should copy involves head position. He sets his eyes directly over the ball. Tiger's former teacher John Anselmo believes this position helps Sergio employ an on-line stroke. I agree, considering that two-time PGA champion, the late Paul Runyan, said that oculists had informed him that this starting position makes it easier to see the straight putting line. Nevertheless, you still should experiment on the practice putting green to see if you putt better with your eyes behind the ball and over the target line. Many great putters, most notably Jack Nicklaus, putt this way.

What you want to guard against is setting your eyes well inside the target line. This position, as John Daly and Phil Mickelson discovered, forces you to swing the putter on such an overly flat backswing path that it's difficult to deliver the putter's face square to the ball consistently. Besides, as short game guru Dave Pelz told me when I worked on a putting article with him for *Golf Magazine*: "The easiest path of the putter to duplicate is the straight back–straight through stroke, simply because the putterhead never leaves the path that runs along the target line."

What I like most about Sergio's setup is his erect posture. By reducing the flex in his knees, bending only slightly from the waist, and letting his arms extend naturally, he alleviates body tension that often causes a player to make an overly slow, extra-short back stroke and a super-fast down stroke. In turn, these faults lead to poor distance control.

Setting up like Sergio will allow you to make a tension-free stroke and pace the ball the proper distance to the hole.

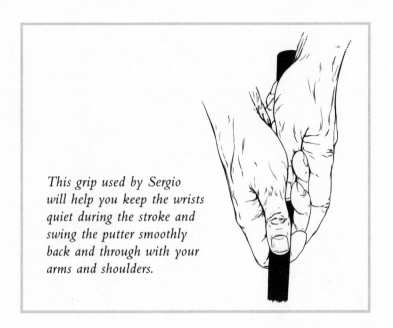

This grip used by Sergio will help you keep the wrists quiet during the stroke and swing the putter smoothly back and through with your arms and shoulders.

One more thing that helps Sergio make a pure, on-line, pendulum stroke is his grip. He grips the club predominantly in the palm of the left hand, so that hand acts as the fulcrum of the stroke, and in the fingers of the right hand to promote more sensitivity or feel. Sergio also drapes the forefinger of his left hand over the fingers of his right hand to promote a wrist-free stroke. Furthermore, he points both thumbs straight down the clubshaft to help maintain a square clubface position from the start of the stroke to its finish.

SERGIO'S PUTTING STROKE

Keeping the body steady promotes a steady and reliable putting stroke.

Through trial-and-error practice, and tips from his golf pro father, Sergio learned that one link to employing a low-back and

Steadiness of body and steadiness of stroke are the characteristic earmarks of Sergio's putting action.

low-through stroke is keeping the body dead still and the wrists locked while swinging the putter solely with the imaginary triangle formed by the arms and shoulders.

"I have never seen a player stay so locked in as Sergio Garcia during the entire stroke," said Gerald McCullagh, one of *Golf Magazine*'s top one hundred teachers in America. "This is one chief reason why he repeatedly swings the putter low along the target line, using a pure pendulum action, and rolls the ball smoothly across the green."

Although Sergio's grip provides him with a sense of unity in the hands, the left hand serves as the guide hand while the right hand provides the power. To encourage each hand to act according to these job descriptions, grip the club more firmly in the left hand (7 on a 1–10 scale) and lightly with the right hand (4 on a 1–10 scale). The longer the putt, the more you should feel the left hand bring the club through the ball and the more forceful the sense of pushing with your right hand.

When Sergio swings into impact, the bottom, or "sole," of the putterhead practically brushes against the putting surface. Consequently, the ball does not skid or bounce off the putterface, as is the case with players who swing the putterhead upward through impact.

Another thing that separates Sergio from other golfers is how he controls the speed of the putt. Unlike other pros, he chooses simply to accelerate the arms a little faster, rather than swing the putter back farther. I prefer Sergio's method of increasing the tempo of the stroke because it's difficult to match the perfect-length stroke to a particular length of putt.

Last but not least, Sergio chooses to "die" the ball into the hole rather than charge the cup. Jack Nicklaus has putted this way all his life, and he's holed miles and miles of putts. Surely Garcia will follow in this great golfer's footsteps.

Why Sergio Is Such a Great Golfer

Sergio possesses an uncanny ability to read the lie, pick the right club, and play the right shot.

• • •

Sergio is as much of a creative genius as fellow Spaniard Pablo Picasso, only he uses a golf club instead of a paintbrush.

• • •

Sergio can play a variety of chips and bunker shots with a sand wedge, from good, bad, and ugly lies, just by making some innovative setup and swing changes.

Sergio's wedge game is so versatile that he can play a spinner that lands on the green and spins back to the hole, a parachute that lands extra softly, or a pitch and roll that flies low and rolls to the hole as smoothly as a putt.

On short putts, Sergio employs a pure pendulum, straight-back, straight-through arms-shoulders stroke.

. . .

On long putts, Sergio simply accelerates his arms, rather than lengthening his stroke.

133

5 • Prep School

Sergio proves that proper preparation promotes peak performance.

Sergio Garcia

knows that practice and preparation are two keys to becoming a better golfer.

Golf is a very fickle sport, owing to the complexities of the swing, an action that takes only one and a half seconds from start to finish but demands that a lot go right for the ball to be struck powerfully and accurately. Furthermore, the conditions of the course change as frequently as one's swing tempo, timing, and rhythm. When you consider that even a small change in a golfer's mental and physical states, from one day to the next, can have a big effect on his or her performance, either in a positive or negative way, you will start realizing that good golf requires you to do much more than simply hit balls at the range.

Hitting a golf ball squarely and solidly has been compared to playing the lottery. I think this is an exaggeration of the critically minded; nevertheless there is some truth to golf not being an easy sport. In fact, Ben Hogan said he only hit one perfect shot per round. Regardless, you can still learn to have control over your swing and hit many good shots during a round of golf.

Most country club golfers only get the chance to play one day on the weekend, but that's not the reason so many players post high scores. The reason they fail to improve is that, during off time away from the course they do not practice, or if they do, it is usually to try a new tip that they hope will turn their driving game around. Most players don't care about practicing the total game, checking their equipment, and doing such important things as working on building body strength and flexibility.

Don't think for a second that Sergio Garcia evolved into the golfer he is today without preparing hard, on and off the course. Sure he hits balls, practicing every conceivable shot, and he works out in the PGA Tour's on-site trailer, but his prep-work regimen is much fuller and involves an extensive number of elements. Why? To paraphrase the great inventor Thomas Edison: "Genius is five percent being born with a gift and ninety-five percent hard work."

If you want to learn to play good golf or lower your existing handicap, it's essential that you learn to sacrifice some playing hours for practice hours, and seriously commit yourself to doing some solid prep work that involves much more than hitting shots before the round on the practice tee or away from the course at the driving range. If you are really serious about shaving strokes off your score, you also should work on building body strength and flexibility, improving your course management skills, strengthening your mental game, and going so far as to do some "armchair practice" when the round is over. Sit quietly and analyze your day's golf, the objective being to focus in on the weak points of your swing and the shots you need to work on. After playing eighteen holes, try to make time to go to the practice area and work on fixing a faulty action in your swing, like a body sway on the backswing or an over-the-top move on the downswing. When pressed for time, at least make a note of your faults so you can work on them the next time you go to the driving range.

Golf fans and members of the press are quick to call Sergio a "phenom," a moniker they also have given to Tiger. The fact is, these two superstars share one common admirable trait: They both began swinging before they were four years old, and ever since have worked diligently to understand the elements of a good swing and creative shot-making. Growing up, they devoted hours and hours to practice until they were able to consistently repeat a good swing action and hit a variety of shots. Of course, both Sergio and Tiger were lucky enough to have fathers who taught them good habits.

In addition, they were given the freedom to personalize their own techniques and shot-making methods.

Though Earl Woods, Tiger's father, was a low-handicap player, Victor Garcia was a golf pro, which explains why Sergio is considered a more inventive shot-maker than Tiger. Sergio has a swing that's compared to Hogan's, the greatest ball striker of all time, and a shot-making game that experts say is better than that of his legendary countryman Seve Ballesteros. These qualities have already allowed Sergio to beat Tiger, and what's made him great will make him even greater and allow him to win major championships.

Playing good golf requires constantly checking the state of your game. You should evaluate your equipment, body strength and flexibility, setup, shot-making skills, distance control, direction control, short game, mental attitude, and course management strategies to pinpoint weak areas of your game and correct them. Sergio is disciplined to do this on a regular basis, and you should be, too, because a "check and correct" system is the only shortcut to playing good golf consistently.

What follows are tips for getting your game in shape via a very specific preparation program that uses Sergio as the ideal model, and covers everything from equipment to improving your green-reading skills.

EQUIPMENT PREPARATION

Sergio constantly experiments with new drivers to see if a new one works better in terms of producing more powerfully accurate shots. Recently, in fact, Sergio switched from Titleist clubs to TaylorMade, based on a higher degree of performance. You should do the same, making sure, most of all, that the shaft on your driver matches your strength and swing speed, the loft built into the clubface matches your swing plane, and your grips match the size of your hands.

In practice, if you notice that the ball is flying low and to the right, chances are the clubshafts are too stiff. You should probably gear back to medium-flex shafts. If you already have medium shafts and the ball still flies low, either the grips on your clubs are too thick for your size hands or you need to swing a more lofted driver, around 10 degrees.

Sergio drives with a TaylorMade R580 club featuring 8.5 degrees of loft and a "rifle" extra-stiff shaft flex.

Since the sand wedge is the second most important club in a player's bag, you should make sure the bounce in your wedge is shallow enough to be used easily off tight fairway lies and matches the type of sand at your club. According to the editors of *Golf Magazine,* in average sand you should use a sand wedge featuring a bounce of 12 degrees, in hard sand a bounce of 10 degrees, and in soft sand a bounce of 14 degrees.

Sergio plays with a TaylorMade RAC sand wedge, featuring 54 degrees of loft and a medium degree of bounce that works well on the many courses he plays while traveling around the world to tournament sites. This club not only features the ideal bounce for hitting shots off sand and fairway grass, it features specially engineered "dual draft" grooves that allow Sergio to attain better distance control. For these reasons, check with your local golf pro to see what he thinks is the best sand wedge for you to carry relative to the type of course you play (e.g., one with soft sand and tightly mowed fairways).

Proper equipment preparation also includes choosing a putter that promotes confidence, matches your hand position at address,

Testing out different drivers featuring different shaft flexes and loft angles is something Sergio and other top pros do constantly. They are always looking to get the "edge" on a fellow player.

and features the proper degree of loft. Playing with a putter that is not custom-fit is sure to cause you to miss putts.

If you're a golfer who likes to set your hands ahead of the ball slightly, play with a putter with added loft. That way, you compensate for decreasing the effective loft of your putter at impact due to your hands finishing ahead of the ball. If you like to set your hands behind the ball slightly at address, play with a putter featuring a low degree of loft. That way, you will compensate for increasing the effective loft of the putter due to making an upswing stroke through impact because of your hands-back position.

Sergio sets his hands in line with the ball at address, so his Taylor-Made Rossa Modena putter, featuring 2.5 degrees of loft, suits him well. However, since he constantly checks his game and makes subtle switches to his setup and stroke, don't be a bit surprised to see him switch to a different TaylorMade putter that allows him to hole more putts.

EXERCISE PREPARATION

Sergio has always been athletic. In fact, doing such things as kicking a soccer ball around and running around the tennis court has had a big effect on his golf swing.

"As a kid, I played a lot of running sports that helped strengthen my legs," said Sergio in the May 2003 issue of *Golf Magazine*. "Now they help me with my golf game, starting with my backswing. Although my arms and shoulders move the club to the top, my legs generate the coil—and that's where I get my power."

You need to become very conscientious about making a regular exercise program part of your preparation process. Jogging is ideal for strengthening your legs, while swinging a weighted club will make you more flexible and thus enhance your turning power.

SETUP PREPARATION

To become good at the game and evolve into a more advanced shot-maker, you must also work constantly on your pre-shot routine. Sergio steps into the ball right foot first, then sets the club-face perpendicular to the target. From this starting position, you will find it easier to take your address and establish a good foundation for swinging on the correct path and plane.

Whether you set up with your feet, knees, hips, and shoulders square to the target line, like Sergio, or play better from an open or closed address position, work on your routine and check your address position regularly in a mirror or on video, or have a playing partner or pro take a look at your starting position. It is easy to slip into a faulty setup.

The setup may not sound important or may seem boring, but the fact is it is very important.

"When you repeat the same routine, your subconscious mind is more apt to let you employ the best swing you grooved in practice," says sports psychologist Dr. Fran Pirozzolo. "Conversely, if you get out of your routine, you will be thrown off your natural rhythm, employ an off-plane action, and be likely to hit an off-line shot."

When it comes to your address, don't be afraid to experiment either, particularly if your shots are not flying on target. It could be that your natural swing is more geared to playing a fade or a draw than a straight shot. Fade-shooters will do better playing from an open-stance setup, and draw-shooters from a closed-stance setup.

When preparing to set up, step into the shot right foot first,
then put the club down square to the target.

SHOT-MAKING PREPARATION

Good drives are very important to good scoring, but the art to scoring depends on much more than driving prowess, as Sergio learned from his father's example and his own playing experience.

Beyond keeping his own personal swing grooved, a smart golfer like Sergio works regularly on his entire tee-to-green game, practicing everything from fairway metal shots, to long irons, to medium irons, to a variety of short-game shots and putts. In fact, Sergio's greatest emphasis is on the short-game shots reviewed in chapter four. But he doesn't just practice standard pitch shots, chips, bunker shots, and putts. He practices shots from funky lies and works on inventing new shots with and without his father's help.

You'd be surprised how many new shots you can learn just from moving the ball back or forward in your stance, opening and closing the clubface, and leaning your weight left or right.

DISTANCE AND DIRECTION CONTROL PREPARATION

Part of your preparation process should also be to work on direction control, particularly with irons and the putter. These clubs require more precision than power, so you can easily become vulnerable if you do not figure out ways to stay on top of your game.

Sergio chokes down on the grip more with irons than with a driver to aid his control. He also plays irons off the heel of the club

*Here, Sergio practices a shot off threadbare sandy turf, knowing
he has to be prepared for any lie on the golf course.*

rather than the sweet spot. This is one of his secrets to hitting such super-accurate iron shots that sit down softly on the green. When this young Spaniard gets on a roll, he knocks down pins the same way Ben Hogan and Johnny Miller used to. Like Sergio, both of these golfing greats used this setup key to control direction and distance on their iron shots, so give this position a try and work on developing a swing tempo that allows you to hit the ball a consistent distance with each club in your bag. For example, if you hit your seven-iron 150 yards on average, make sure that when doing off-course prep work you match that mean distance. If not, work on fixing your tempo. If your shots are flying too far, slow your swing down. If your shots are finishing well short of your target, speed up your tempo slightly.

If your distance control is off on putts, you're probably exaggerating wrist action. Tame the wrists and promote a pure arms-shoulders-controlled pendulum stroke by practicing with a long putter, as Sergio has done. Putting with your eyes closed and trying to hole putts from, say, 20 feet, will also help to improve your distance control.

It you have a problem hitting putts on the correct line, practice putting with the toe of the putterhead. This unorthodox practice drill will help you correct a faulty out-to-in or in-to-out stroke and groove a straight-back-and-straight-through action.

This process is part of the check-and-correct system I mentioned earlier, and one reason why Sergio and other top pros play so well so often.

You will only be able to handle a course situation like this—short iron to a plateau green surrounded by trouble—if, like Sergio, you work on finding a swing tempo that allows you to hit the ball straight and the same distance with a particular club.

146

MENTAL ATTITUDE PREPARATION

One of the qualities I admire about Sergio's game is his positive mental attitude. No matter how he played the day before, he approaches each new round with an air of confidence. For this reason, I agree with sports psychologist Glen Albaugh, who believes that a player does not have to be playing well to become confident. By changing your attitude and seeing the glass as half full rather than half empty, you can help your golf. The more confident you are, the more energy you will be willing to devote to a shot, and the better the result.

"Confidence can be a matter of choice, when it is a way of being not related to the outcome of a previous performance," said Albaugh. "To further understand this definition of confidence, consider separating it, with external and internal confidence having distinctly different meanings. While external confidence (the kind we hear about the most) is based upon the success of previous repetitions or game performances, internal confidence is developed systematically through positive self-talk, positive imagery, physical posture, and trust. Through practice of these concepts, internal confidence can become an acquired skill. Internal confidence begins with an unwavering belief that your method-technique is correct. The swing you have is the only one you will play with today. It is a conscious decision to go with what you have. Confidence demands that you be your own best friend. If we can control what we say to others, we can control what we say to ourselves. Positive self-talk is a matter of choice. After a belief in oneself and positive self-talk have been developed, positive imagery follows. Trust comes next, as the infinite wisdom of a body/mind. Trust entails giving up conscious control and is facilitated, in part, by internal confidence."

One chief reason why Sergio plays such great shots on the course is that once he leaves the practice tee, he lets go mentally, depending less on the conscious mind and more on the subconscious to take control of his action. Doing this requires a tremendous amount of trust that only comes from preparing the correct way when off the course. In a nutshell, the more you practice, the more you get to know your swing, the more you get to trust your swing, and the less you have to think about what you are doing technically.

COURSE MANAGEMENT PREPARATION

Sergio has learned to become a great course manager through playing practice rounds and testing out strategies. Rather than take silly chances on the course, he's now mature enough to pick a long iron off the tee on a narrow hole bordered by extreme trouble areas, and to play a shot safely back to the fairway from deep rough, instead of going for the green. You, too, should discipline yourself, through preparation in practice, to take shot-making risks only if the odds are in your favor.

Being a good course manager also means learning how to prepare for a putt by applying good green-reading skills.

The secret to reading greens well is staying alert and aware from the time your approach shot hits the green until you set up to putt. If you watch Sergio play, you'll see he's always looking around, almost like a wild animal checking out the surroundings for prey. He's super-alert, as you should be.

As you approach a green, keep an eye out for the lay of the land surrounding the putting surface. In hilly areas, a green may be built into a sloping piece of land, for instance, with a right-to-left slope.

The green itself may appear level because it contrasts with the sloping terrain around you. However, in most cases, in reality the green will be sloping somewhat right to left also. It's fairly difficult to notice this once you're on the green, but as you approach the putting green you can visually pick up this information quite easily.

When you read the green, determine the line of the putt by looking at the line from behind the ball, from behind the hole, and from both sides of the target line. Sergio usually reads the break from behind the hole, but if not he stalks the area around the target line until he is sure of which way the ball will break. Give yourself the same flexibility. View the line from different angles until you are sure of the break and how much curve you must allow for. Keep in mind if you have a putt that's flat at the start with a break later along the line, the putt will break more than if the opposite condition is true—when the line slopes early but then flattens out around the hole. This is because early in the roll of the putt, the ball rolls faster, with more energy, and will not be affected by the pull of gravity caused by any side slope. The effect of any slope will be much greater if it occurs nearer the hole, when the ball slows down and is thus much more susceptible to the force of gravity.

One paramount key to reading greens as well as Sergio is being able to judge their speed. Many golfers fail to understand this important putting variable, but being able to predict how fast or slow the ball will roll across a green plays an important role in determining the amount of break in a green's surface and the actual strength of the stroke needed. In short, if a green is super-quick, a putt will break far more than a putt over the same amount of slope on a slow green, and vice versa.

The grain of the green may affect the break as well as the speed of the putt, particularly if you putt on coarse Bermuda grass greens, common in Florida and elsewhere in the southern United States.

Although young, Sergio is a smart, well-prepared player who has learned to be disciplined enough to select a long iron on a very narrow hole (above) and to play a shot back to the fairway from a very bad lie in rough (facing page).

Sergio takes his time reading a green, knowing that if he reads the break correctly he will give himself the best chance to hole the putt, and if he doesn't, he'll probably miss the putt.

If, for example, you face a right-to-left putt and the grain runs right-to-left, the putt will break more than you think just from judging the slope. If the grain grows in the opposite direction to the line of the putt, the putt will normally break less than you think.

The best, most efficient way to check for grain direction in the grass is to look closely at the edge of the cup. If you see a ragged or ruffled edge, that's the side of the hole the grain is growing toward. If the ragged side is on the right of the hole, the ball will break a shade more to the right, and just the opposite if the ragged side is to the left.

Becoming a good grain-reader has a lot to do with experience. Sergio has played all over the world, so he has a lot of information stored in his mind's data bank about how to putt on different greens. I'm not suggesting that you become a globe-trotting golfer to lower your handicap; however, the more courses you play the more you will enhance your green-reading skills, relative to judging speed and break. Seeing a variety of putting surfaces and staying alert to all the factors just reviewed will sharpen your green-reading skills so that you know what direction to hit every putt and how hard to stroke the ball.

Why Sergio Is Such a Great Golfer

Sergio prepares by analyzing the flight and shot pattern of his clubs, particularly the driver, to determine what shaft and degree of loft allow him to hit the ball powerfully and accurately.

. . .

Sergio prepares to hit standard shots by stepping into the setup right foot first, then aligning the clubface perpendicular to the target before jockeying his body into a more reliable "square" position.

. . .

Sergio's preparation process includes trying to invent new shots.

• • •

Sergio prepares for a tournament by working hard on direction and distance control, knowing the importance of landing

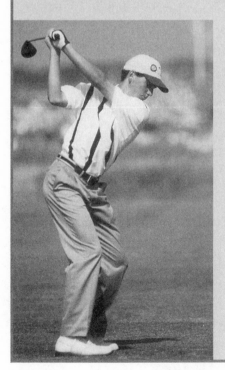

the ball in the right area of fairway to set up an attacking approach shot, and on a particular area of the green to set up an aggressive birdie putt.

• • •

Sergio's prep work includes practicing hitting long irons off the tee on narrow holes and hitting shots from deep rough back to the fairway.

• • •

Sergio prepares by putting on different types of greens to learn how the ball reacts on sloping surfaces featuring such grasses as Bermuda.

Acknowledgments

I thank my agent, Scott Waxman, and also Rob McMahon at Putnam's for agreeing with me that it was due time an instructional book was written about the youngest superstar in golf, Sergio Garcia.

As you now can appreciate, the focal point of *Play Like Sergio Garcia* is an in-depth analysis of Sergio's phenomenal swing and shot-making game. However, in unraveling the mysteries of Sergio's unique techniques, I did not rely only on my own former experience as a golf teacher and what I learned from a sixteen-year stint as senior instruction editor for *Golf Magazine*. I depended, too, on insights from the game's top teachers affiliated with the PGA of America and the United States Golf Teachers Federation, and further, on the opinions of my fellow golf writers, professional golf analysts from various television networks, and experts from The Golf Channel. And I could not have done such a good job of analyzing Sergio's game had I not received from Robert Kraut, of The Booklegger, a video of the 1999 PGA Championship. Being able to play this and press the pause button time and time again allowed me to more easily dissect Sergio's swing down to the bone and pass on what I learned to you.

As you now know, Sergio's swing is unorthodox, but even more efficient and effective than the one once employed by legendary ballstriker Ben Hogan. Therefore, I needed superb photographs and lifelike illustrations to convey the instructional message to you. I'm extremely grateful to world-renowned golf photographer Phil Sheldon for coming to the rescue and providing such wonderful images,

including one he received as a gift from Sergio showing him swinging at age three. I also owe thanks to artist Shu Kuga for his wonderful drawings, particularly those that help the reader see the similarities
and differences between the Garcia and Hogan swings.

I'm indebted to guru swing coach Jim McLean for writing the
foreword to this book and offering keen observations about Sergio's
swing.

Last but not least, I thank you, the reader, for being interested
enough to make an investment in this book that I'm sure will pay off.

Index

Note: *Italics* indicate illustrations.